AMERICA'S FIRST LADIES

CHANGING EXPECTATIONS

To the memory of Menasha Tausner,
a much beloved Feinberg family friend

Photographs ©: cover: Superstock, Madison; Folio, Clinton; JFK Library (Mark Shaw), Kennedy; AP/Wide World Photos: cover (Roosevelt), 62, 85, 107; Corbis-Bettmann: 20, 39, 44, 77; Folio, Inc.: 48 (Patricia Lanza), 57 (Fred J. Maroon), 99, 114 (Michael Patrick), 66, 123; Gamma-Liaison: 128 (Roger Sandler); Gerald R. Ford Library: 93; John F. Kennedy Library: cover top right, 28; Ken Hawkins: 53; Library of Congress: 11, 34, 55, 90 (Jay Mallin Photos); National Archives: 104; Retna Ltd./Camera Press Ltd.: 40 (Jacques Lowe); Ronald Reagan Library: 69; Superstock: cover top left; Sygma: 82 (Arthur Grace), 9 (Ira Wyman); UPI/Corbis-Bettmann: 46, 119;

Library of Congress Cataloging-in-Publication Data

Feinberg, Barbara Silberdick.
America's first ladies: changing expectations / by Barbara Silberdick Feinberg.
p. cm. — (Democracy in action)
Includes bibliographical references and index.
Summary: Traces the evolution of America's First Ladies from the role of White House hostess to that of social and political leader.
ISBN: 0-531-11379-5
1. President's spouses—United States—Juvenile literature.
[1. First ladies.] I. Title II. Series: Democracy in action (Franklin Watts, Inc.)
E176.2.F45   1998
973'.09'9—dc21
97-34955
CIP
AC

AMERICA'S FIRST LADIES

CHANGING EXPECTATIONS

BARBARA
SILBERDICK
FEINBERG

FRANKLIN WATTS
A Division of Grolier Publishing

New York, London, Hong Kong, Sydney
Danbury, Connecticut

CONTENTS

ACKNOWLEDGMENTS

I am grateful to Naomi and David Neft for getting me personal copies of some of the out-of-print books I needed for my research. I appreciate the assistance of Catherine Sewell, archivist at the Ronald Reagan Library who located information for me about the volume of mail Nancy Reagan received. I would like to thank editor, Lorna Greenberg, for her thoughtful comments and encouragement while I was preparing the manuscript. I am very indebted to editor Brendan January for his skill in carefully cutting paragraphs and pages so as to produce a book of manageable length.

A NOTE TO THE READER

This book discusses the many functions First Ladies have performed and the way they have reflected and sometimes changed the status of women in American society. It does not delve at any length into the personal lives of the presidential wives, but such information is readily available and is well worth reading. Many First Ladies have written intriguing autobiographies of their early years and their experiences in the White House. These works provide interesting details about their lives and times that could not be included in a book of this length. In addition, a number of authors have written biographies of the presidents' wives and some have compiled anthologies of First Ladies' lives. Some of these titles are listed in the chapter notes. The rest can be found in library catalogues. Also beyond the scope of this book are accounts of presidential relatives who sometimes assumed the social responsibilities of First Ladies. Some took charge to help those presidents who were widowers or who, in one case, never married. Others substituted for presidential wives who were unwilling or unable to take up their public responsibilities at the White House. A list of the First Ladies, including their lifespans, husbands, and the years they served, can be found in the Appendix.

ONE

SETTING AN EXAMPLE FOR AMERICAN WOMEN

*"I will neither keep house
nor make butter."*

—*Sarah Polk*

On June 1, 1990, the major television networks carried a live broadcast of graduation ceremonies at Wellesley College, a women's college in eastern Massachusetts. First Lady Barbara Bush and Raisa Gorbachev, wife of the Soviet leader, were giving commencement speeches to the 600 graduates and their 5,000 relatives and guests. Ordinarily, a First Lady's graduation remarks do not make newspaper headlines or preempt regularly scheduled television programming, but on this sunny, hot day, the public eagerly waited to hear what white-haired, grandmotherly Mrs. Bush would say. The choice of Barbara Bush as Wellesley's commencement speaker had generated a well-publicized controversy on campus that had spilled over into the media. Even if Mrs. Gorbachev had not accompanied her, it is likely that her speech would have received widespread coverage.

In April, about 150 seniors, a quarter of the graduating class, had signed a petition protesting the invitation to the First Lady to participate in their commencement exercises. The students wanted a speaker whose personal achievements mirrored their own aspirations, who had an advanced degree or a challenging career, and who was valued for her own attainments, not those of her husband or family. From their feminist perspective, Mrs. Bush was unsuitable. Peggy Reid, co-sponsor of the petition, explained:

> The plain and simple fact is that Barbara Bush was not chosen as a speaker because of her commendable role as a mother; nor was she chosen for her admirable volunteer work. If such were the case, why were other equally dedicated mothers and community volunteers not chosen?
>
> . . . Barbara Bush was selected because of her husband's accomplishments and notoriety, not those of her own. So it is not the validity of her choices in life that we are calling into question, but rather the fact that we are honoring not Barbara Bush, but Mrs. George Bush.[1]

Despite Reid's comments, the seniors did appear to be criticizing "her choices in life." Writers and columnists all over the nation debated the issue the students had raised. Later, at the commencement ceremony, one-third of the graduating class wore purple armbands to "celebrate all the unknown women who have dedicated their lives to the service of others."[2]

In the 1990s, women expected to have it all: a profession, a husband, and children. In 1945, when she was a nineteen-year-old sophomore, Barbara Bush dropped out of Smith College, a women's college in western Massachusetts, to marry George Bush. She soon became a busy wife and mother who found time to do volunteer work for charities but never completed her education. In those days, American women were supposed to find fulfillment as homemakers. Could Barbara Bush offer a message that was relevant to the graduating class of 1990?

When the Wellesley protest erupted, she told her staff that she did not want to "complain, explain, or apologize in any way. . . . I wanted the students to consider: You have to get involved in something larger than yourself; Remember to get joy out of life; Cherish human relationships."[3] These themes dominated all her graduation speeches in 1990 and received little attention until she visited the Wellesley campus.

*Barbara Bush won over a skeptical crowd of college graduates
with a friendly demeanor and a great punch line.*

There she told her audience that "we are in a transitional period right now . . . learning to adjust to the changes and choices we .
. . men and women. . . are facing."[4] Adjustment required an acceptance of diversity and respect for others' life choices even though
they might be different from one's own. Although she was addressing young women seeking meaningful careers, she defended traditional family values. "At the end of your life, you will never regret
not having passed one more test, not winning one more verdict, or
not closing one more deal. You will regret time not spent with a
husband, a friend, a child, or a parent."[5] She received a standing
ovation. Most commentators found her remarks at Wellesley far
more appealing and interesting than Mrs. Gorbachev's impersonal
speech, which focused on greater openness in the Soviet Union

and friendship among nations. Although the graduates may have considered Barbara Bush an old-fashioned wife and mother, they appreciated her heartfelt comments about the life choices they would be making.

HILLARY CLINTON HAS IT ALL?

During the 1992 presidential race, Wellesley students and alumnae had reason to rejoice when one of their own, Hillary Rodham Clinton, a member of the class of 1969, campaigned on behalf of her husband, Bill Clinton. The students knew she had combined marriage, parenthood, and a career. A member of the baby-boom generation, Hillary had come of age during the turbulent 1960s and had received a law degree from Yale University in 1973. Hillary became the first female partner at the prestigious Rose law firm in Little Rock, Arkansas. She was also actively involved in the Children's Defense Fund and managed to raise daughter Chelsea while attending to her duties as the governor's wife. She even kept her own last name for the first seven years of her marriage—until she concluded that it might hurt her husband's 1982 gubernatorial reelection campaign.

To many observers, Hillary's activities as a working mother were a liability when Bill Clinton ran for president in 1992. Former President Richard Nixon stated, "Barbara Bush plays the piano so she doesn't drown out George's violin. Hillary pounds the piano so hard that Bill can't be heard. You want a wife who's intelligent, but not too intelligent."[6] As Nixon predicted, Hillary became a target for criticism during the 1992 campaign. In March, an article in the *Washington Post* had pointed out that Hillary's career seriously compromised her husband's impartiality in office. Through Hillary, the Rose law firm exercised undue influence over the Arkansas governor. At stake were the interests of Rose clients in the regulation of the poultry industry, in rules governing the way corporations treated shareholders, and in the enforcement of environmental controls. The article claimed that Hillary was vulnerable to charges of conflict of interest between the competing demands of her professional life and the performance of her official duties as a governor's wife.[7]

Responding to reporters, Mrs. Clinton said she had done everything possible to avoid conflicts of interest and focused instead on

Sarah Polk was a trusted advisor and confidante for her husband.

the difficult choices facing modern women. Losing her self-control, she snapped, "I suppose I could have stayed home and baked cookies and had teas, but what I decided to do is fulfill my profession, which I entered before my husband was in public life."[8] This comment was widely publicized and did little to endear Mrs. Clinton to the homemakers and mothers of America.

Hillary was not the first candidate's wife to make homemaking a lesser priority. During the political campaign of 1844, Sarah Polk was chided that Mrs. Henry Clay, the wife of her husband's opponent, would make a better First Lady because she was an economical housekeeper and could make good butter. Sarah retorted, "If I get to the White House, I expect to live on $25,000 a year [the president's salary then] and I will neither keep house nor make butter."[9] At that time, women were judged largely on their appearance and domestic skills. As First Lady, Sarah kept her word and privately served as President James Polk's political assistant.

Bill Clinton's campaign advisors urged Hillary to soften her statements about her career and appear as a more supportive and loving wife. So Hillary used her commencement address to the 1992 graduating class at Wellesley to make amends to the wives and mothers she had offended by including homemaking as one of the options available to women. "You may choose to be a corporate executive or a rocket scientist, you may run for public office, you may choose to stay home and raise your children—but you can now make any or all of those choices—and they can be the work of your life," she told them.[10] As a First Lady, Hillary chose to become an active member of her husband's presidential administration and to have an independent job. In 1995 she began writing a syndicated newspaper column, and she authored a book championing family life, donating the proceeds to charity. The criticism Barbara Bush faced for not having a career and the accusations made against Hillary Clinton because she did have a profession reflect ongoing tensions in American society as more and more wives and mothers enter the workplace. The issue became important because First Ladies are expected to set examples for American women. Will a First Lady be an acceptable role model in the twenty-first century if she focuses her energy solely on helping her husband to do his job? If she already has a career and continues to work outside the White House? If she is content to remain a wife and mother?

Only one other First Lady continued to pursue an independent career after her husband became president. For the more than twelve years that she was First Lady, Eleanor Roosevelt managed to write a daily newspaper column, host a weekly radio program, tour twice a year as a professional lecturer, pen columns for two magazines, and write an autobiography—while fulfilling her obligations at the White House. After her husband's first term in the White House, Eleanor's interests shifted. She relinquished her partnership in Val-Kill Industries, which made furniture, and in the Todhunter School of Manhattan, where she had taught when her husband was governor of New York. Her considerable earnings were donated to charity. During World War II, she became the first presidential wife to accept an official government post, deputy-director of the Office of Civilian Defense. This indefatigable woman also found time to perform her traditional duties as First Lady as well as those her husband Franklin assigned to her.

Of course, she had critics. One newspaper commented that "the fact remains that being the first lady of the land is a full-time job in itself and that the dignity of the President and of the country cannot but suffer when his name is used for commercial purposes."[11] Eleanor did not intend to give up working. She explained, "What some people do not seem to understand is that I am really not doing anything that I haven't done for a long time. It's only Franklin's position that has brought them to the attention of people."[12]

AMBIGUOUS RESPONSIBILITIES AND CHANGING REALITIES

Being a presidential wife is not an easy task. For all that First Ladies may do, they are not even mentioned in the Constitution, and the job description accompanying their title is ill-defined. They are in effect unpaid government workers whose duties more or less depend on their individual personalities, interests, and the amount of power they are able to exercise. Furthermore, they lose their privacy and frequently face scrutiny and criticism from the media. Their reactions to this situation are as diverse as the ladies themselves. For the most part, they accept that they are national figures and must sometimes sacrifice their personal pursuits to public concerns.

As the nation's first presidential wife, Martha Washington chafed under the restraints. Having run a plantation, joined her husband at military camps, and received gifts and honors in her own right from a grateful nation, this First Lady objected to the restrictive rules of protocol (proper social behavior) and precedents (who goes first) she had to obey. The rules were designed to ensure that the new head of state and his wife were treated with honor and respect. She wrote from New York, the nation's first capital, "I live a very dull life here and know nothing that passes in town. I never go to any public place . . . indeed, I am more like a state prisoner than anything else. There are certain boundaries set for me which I must not depart from . . . and . . . I cannot do as I like."[13] It was considered undignified for her to visit friends or dine at their homes.

Martha was referred to as Lady Washington, not the First Lady. Although the new American republic had successfully rebelled against a monarchy, it still used the vocabulary of royalty as a sign of respect for its leaders and their wives. In the early nineteenth century, such pretensions of nobility were replaced with more democratic terms of address. The wives of the nation's chief executives were called "Mrs. President" and "Presidentress." The term "First Lady" was introduced in 1849 at the funeral of Dolley Madison during President Zachary Taylor's tribute to the gracious presidential hostess. It was commonly used to refer to the president's wife by the time Abraham and Mary Lincoln presided over the White House. In the 1960s, however, Jackie Kennedy did not want to be called First Lady, preferring the simpler Mrs. Kennedy. She felt the by-now traditional title was better suited to a racehorse.[14]

Like Martha Washington, many First Ladies had difficulty adjusting to the demands of their position. A few felt inadequate, some found it hard to repress their own personalities or interests, while others resented the loss of their privacy. For example, invalid Eliza Johnson, a shoemaker's daughter from the Tennessee mountains, suffered from tuberculosis and was unable to provide for White House entertaining. When her husband Andrew became president in 1865, the new First Lady remarked, "[I]t's all very well for those who like it—but I do not like this public life at all. I often wish the time would come when we could return to where I feel we best belong."[15]

In the 1920s, many women experienced a new sense of freedom and demonstrated their independence from established social rules by cutting their hair short and smoking cigarettes in public. President Calvin Coolidge discouraged his wife from such undignified behavior. The lively, energetic Grace Coolidge, a former teacher, complained, "Being wife to a government worker is a very confining position."[16] In 1945, when Harry Truman succeeded to the presidency upon the death of Franklin Roosevelt, Bess became a very reluctant First Lady. "I am not used to this awful public life," she admitted right after Roosevelt's funeral.[17] Having seen the constant criticism of Eleanor Roosevelt's activities in the press, she limited her official appearances and returned often to her home in Independence, Missouri, to protect her privacy. She told reporters, "I am not the one who is elected. I have nothing to say to the public."[18]

Other women have welcomed the chance to become a First Lady. Some simply enjoyed living in the White House and being treated like royalty. A few felt they deserved this reward because their manipulations and maneuvers made their husbands president. Others found it a wonderful opportunity to be of service to the nation. For instance, Julia Tyler, President John Tyler's young second wife, loved the privileges of being First Lady. "I have commenced my auspicious reign," she wrote soon after her marriage in 1844.[19] She was attended at all times by twelve personal maids of honor and rode around in a carriage drawn by six white horses. She was treated like royalty and even introduced that practice of having "Hail to the Chief" played when the president appeared for official occasions. In the 1870s, Julia Grant, the wife of Civil War victor Ulysses S. Grant, also basked in the pleasure of being First Lady, claiming "My life at the White House was like a bright and beautiful dream.[20]

Some First Ladies used their positions to benefit others. A self-effacing Eleanor Roosevelt claimed that she was only trying to help her husband, to serve "his purposes," but she admitted, "I think I sometimes acted as a spur even though the spurring was not always wanted or welcome."[21] A political activist long before she moved to the White House, Eleanor continued to urge her husband to take action to improve the lives of the poor and the neglected. "A First Lady is in a position to know the needs of the country and do something about them," Rosalynn Carter announced.[22] When her husband, Jimmy Carter, became president in 1977, she became his unofficial partner.

According to one expert, "First Ladies have reflected the status of American women of their time while helping shape expectations of what women can properly do."[23] Traditionally, a First Lady's influence as a role model was limited to serving as hostess for her husband and country, setting fashion trends, turning the White House into a suitable home for her husband and family, raising her children, and protecting her husband's health. Nevertheless, these activities often had political overtones. Modern presidential wives have taken on additional responsibilities. Unlike their predecessors, they actively campaign at election times; publicly support humanitarian, social, and cultural causes; more openly enter into political partnerships with their husbands; and supervise the staff of the Office of First Lady, a group of aides who handle correspondence, scheduling, speechwriting, etc. Their influence does not necessarily end when they leave the White House. While some have resumed their private lives, others have continued to serve the public. As widows, First Ladies have led the nation in mourning their husbands. Most have willingly advised their successors. Whether future First Ladies will delegate some of their duties to others or assume even more obligations remains to be seen. Whatever course they take, they will continue to set an example for the rest of the nation and demonstrate what determined women can do.

▮▮▮▮▮▮▮ TWO ▮▮▮▮▮▮▮▮

ENTERTAINING AT THE WHITE HOUSE

*"Any gentleman or lady of either party,
who chose to visit...were received
with equal civility."*
—Abigail Adams

In 1886, twenty-one-year-old Frances "Frankie" Folsom Cleveland, newly wed to President Grover Cleveland, decided to hold receptions on Saturday afternoons to accommodate working women who usually had the day off. An official urged her to discontinue these social events, but the First Lady refused to comply and ordered the receptions to continue "so long as there were any store clerks, or other self-supporting women and girls who wished to come to the White House."[1] This single act endeared her to women all over the nation. The youngest First Lady in American history was also one of the most compassionate. While Frankie did not back demands for women's voting rights and steered clear of politics, her receptions showed her sensitivity to women's issues.

Like working women, African-Americans were not welcome at the White House, but Lou Hoover, wife of President Herbert Hoover, found that tradition unacceptable. In 1930, she gave a series of teas to honor the wives of members of Congress during her first social season at the White House, as custom dictated. This reserved and unprepossessing First Lady learned that one member of Congress, Republican Congressman Oscar DePriest of Illinois, was black. Washington, D.C., like all Southern cities at that time, was racially segregated, and entertaining the wife of a black congressman could have serious political repercussions. Her staff looked for precedents from past administrations for guidance and discovered that Theodore Roosevelt had been the only president to invite a black person, Booker T. Washington, to the Executive Mansion. Of course, blacks entered the White House regularly to work as domestic servants for presidents and their wives. The decision about Jessie DePriest was postponed while the matter was researched, but Lou was troubled. As a Quaker, she believed that all races were equal and made the courageous decision to act on her beliefs.

On June 12, 1931, Jessie DePriest was finally welcomed at the White House. Lou Hoover gave an extra tea party for her, inviting only those congressional wives who would be comfortable in the presence of a black woman. The White House police, guarding the mansion, were informed to expect a black guest and to allow her admission. Like the rest of Mrs. Hoover's guests, Jessie DePriest spent a few minutes conversing with her in the Green Room and then moved on to the Red Room for a cup of tea. In the opinion of Ike Hoover, chief usher, in charge of the day-to-day running of the White House, Jessie DePriest was "the most composed one in the group."[2]

Jessie DePriest's visit set off a controversy. The Texas State legislature passed a resolution condemning Mrs. Hoover for inviting her, and the newspapers were divided on the wisdom of her decision. The Southern segregationist press was up in arms. Typical was an editorial published in a Mobile Alabama newspaper. "Mrs. Herbert Hoover offered to the South and to the nation an arrogant insult yesterday when she entertained a Negro woman at a White House tea."[3] Yet an editorial in Bristol, Virginia, echoed the sentiments of most of the Northern newspapers, writing, "Politically she put into practice the brotherhood of man"[4]

EIGHTEENTH AND NINETEENTH CENTURY ENTERTAINING

These examples illustrate how two courageous First Ladies tried to depart from traditions established in the earliest days of the republic, when official receptions were usually exclusive, limited to diplomats, officials, and members of the social elite and their guests, noted artists, writers, and inventors, and occasional visitors from out of town. It wasn't until widower Andrew Jackson threw open the doors of the Executive Mansion to ordinary citizens that they were welcomed at the White House, and they trampled the carpets and ruined the fine furnishings. Perhaps this reinforced the undemocratic guest lists of so many nineteenth-century and early twentieth-century First Ladies.

The nation's first hostess, Martha Washington, was aware that she would be setting precedents for the First Ladies who came after her. Her receptions were carefully crafted to establish a dignified atmosphere that would compare favorably to those held by European monarchies. Yet Martha also wished to create an aura of simplicity suitable for a republican system of government. Some of her guests criticized her parties as too informal while others accused her of imitating royalty.

She held staid, formal gatherings on Friday evenings during which Colonel David Humphreys, Washington's assistant, formally announced each guest, a practice continued today but handled by social aides at the White House. Women were expected to curtsy when introduced to Martha, and she acknowledged them by nodding to them. Then Martha seated herself on a sofa while George circulated among the invited government officials and members of society. Light and inexpensive refreshments were served, usually tea, coffee, and cakes. Promptly at nine o'clock, the First Lady rose, establishing the custom that the presidential family retires early, and told her guests, "The General usually retires at nine o'clock, and I usually precede him."[5] Martha also gave receptions on Tuesday afternoons and dinners for government officials on Thursdays.

Having attended Martha's receptions for the eight years that her husband was vice president, Abigail Adams was prepared to follow in Martha's footsteps when she became First Lady in 1797. As the wife and confidante of former diplomat John Adams, and world traveler, however, she was reluctant to make small talk with the ladies, preferring to discuss political affairs with the men. This is why she was perceived by some as intensely partisan. She defended herself in a letter to a newspaper editor, claiming, "Any gentleman or lady of either party, who chose to visit there [at her receptions] were received with equal civility."[6] She was the first president's wife to entertain in the Executive Mansion.

Dolley Madison became extremely influential
in both social and political circles.

Dolley Madison was the first presidential wife to actually enjoy giving parties and receptions, and she had plenty of experience, supervising social events for widowed president Thomas Jefferson and then for her own husband James Madison. She has left her mark on American history as the nation's most celebrated hostess.

She gave the nation's first Inaugural Ball, and from then on, the White House became the center of Washington social life. Dolley's parties, called "drawing rooms," were given every Wednesday evening. No invitations were needed. At past White House receptions, men and women socialized in separate groups, but now they felt free to mingle and talk as they never had before. Conversation flowed, including the latest gossip. Adept at small talk, Dolley insisted, "It is one of the sources of my happiness never to desire knowledge of other people's business."[7] Dolley attracted interesting people to the Executive Mansion, from inventors to writers and artists as well as politicians. Food was plentiful and featured such treats as ice cream. Her political dinners were known for their excellent menus and service; Dolley was equally gracious to her husband's supporters and opponents and never forgot a name or a face, a skill her husband lacked. She was a political asset to him. She became a national asset when the British burned the White House during the War of 1812. She fled to safety only after having saved Gilbert Stuart's portrait of George Washington and important state papers. Her parties soon resumed in the Madisons' temporary Washington residence, the Octagon House.

Under Dolley's social leadership, women became more prominent, appearing at public events, such as sessions of Congress. She also gave parties for the wives of her husbands' cabinet members when their husbands were meeting with the president. Dolley Madison's pleasure hostessing social events even extended to children. As First Lady, she instituted the Easter egg roll for youngsters on the grounds of the Capitol. In 1878, however, Congress passed a law forbidding them from playing on the grounds around the Capitol. For generations, they had rolled Easter eggs down Capitol Hill on Easter Monday. Another First Lady, Lucy Hayes, came to their rescue. "We simply cannot sit idly by and see children disappointed next year," she told her husband.[8] He vetoed the law, while she invited the children to use the lawn around the Executive Mansion for their annual rite.

Social life at the White House declined when Dolley's husband left office. On occasion, lavish parties and balls were given, but weekly receptions were abandoned. Other social customs fell into temporary disuse as well. Elizabeth Monroe, wife of President James Monroe, refused the tedious practice requiring the First Lady and wives of cabinet members to pay brief visits to the wives of incoming members of Congress. Nevertheless, this time-consuming custom continued until Lou Hoover put an end to it. Elizabeth's successor, Louisa Adams, entertained occasionally but kept mostly to herself, writing, "There is something in this great unsocial house which depresses my spirits beyond expression and makes it impossible for me to feel at home or to fancy that I have a home anywhere."[9] As her husband spent more and more time at work than with her, she retreated into depression.

From the 1830s through the 1850s, young ladies began replacing First Ladies as White House hostesses. Widowed president Andrew Jackson and bachelor president James Buchanan had to recruit female relatives to greet their guests, while other presidents had wives who would not or could not entertain. Ailing Elizabeth Monroe, elderly Anna Harrison, paralyzed Letitia Tyler, delicate Margaret Taylor, bookish Abigail Fillmore, and fragile Eliza Johnson all delegated their social duties to their daughters or other family members. Jane Pierce did not socialize because she was in mourning.

Many First Ladies had ailments that prevented them from entertaining at the White House. At the time, it was socially acceptable for them to plead illness as a reason for not serving as their husband's hostesses. Women were seen as the fragile sex. With the exception of well-traveled Elizabeth Monroe and Louisa Adams, many presidential wives also lacked a broad social background and training in the rules of proper social behavior.

In the 1860s, Mary Lincoln entertained in grand style, hoping to gain acceptance from established Washington society and to bolster morale during the Civil War. Mary received members of Congress, diplomats, judges, and the military on New Year's Day and holidays. The public saw her during the traditional spring and winter receptions in the East Room, where as many as 4,000 citizens shook her hand, and souvenir hunters cut away pieces of the White House curtains. To reduce expenses, Mary preferred holding public receptions to formal state dinners. Her husband disagreed until she pointed out that public receptions were more democratic and less elitist, a view consistent with his overall philosophy. Nevertheless, she did give a few formal state dinners, including one to honor visiting French royalty. She chose the menus, supervised the cooking, and arranged floral centerpieces. Despite her cost-cutting concerns, this inconsistent and contradictory First Lady ordered two new sets of expensive china for the White House and found herself criticized as frivolous and extravagant.

In the 1870s, First Lady Julia Grant bought even more china, gave very elaborate parties, and hosted twenty-nine-course state dinners. Yet, she managed to escape public condemnation because the post Civil War years were marked by an industrial boom and the rise of new millionaires who competed to outspend one another in maintaining a luxurious lifestyle. In the late 1880s, Caroline Harrison not only presided graciously over official functions, she went on to organize painting classes for the wives of government officials. She also decorated the first Christmas tree installed in the White House.

Some socially active First Ladies in the nineteenth-century altered White House entertaining to conform to their own views of morality as well as to influence the nation. Because of her religious beliefs, Sarah

Polk banned hard liquor, card-playing, and dancing in the White House. "To dance in these rooms would be undignified," she explained.[10] When her husband left office in 1849, the ban was lifted.

In 1877, President and Mrs. Hayes also entertained with dignity, adding a crest featuring a golden American eagle, to formal White House invitations. Lucy Hayes was the first presidential wife to graduate from college, Cincinnati Wesleyan Female College, but she is remembered for having refused to serve alcoholic beverages at the White House. She and her husband had been dismayed by the amount of drunkenness at Washington gatherings and decided to do something about it. At this time, crusaders, such as the Women's Christian Temperance Union (WCTU), were mobilizing public opinion to condemn drinking liquor, beer, and wine. The WCTU applauded Lucy's ban, but she did not belong to this organization because its members were far too militant to suit her. Others condemned her and gave her the derogatory nickname "Lemonade Lucy." She told her critics, "It is true that I shall violate a precedent; but I shall not violate the Constitution which is all that, through my husband, I have taken an oath to obey."[11]

At the turn of the century, another president's wife was an invalid, but after the 1870s, fragility was no longer an essential part of femininity, and illness was no longer a socially acceptable excuse for First Ladies to shirk their duties. First Lady Ida McKinley, a victim of epilepsy, managed to appear at social occasions, but the McKinleys held few official functions, preferring smaller dinners and teas. Her husband broke with tradition and seated her next to him so that he could place a handkerchief over her face when she had a seizure. She set an example for future First Ladies: Nellie Taft, suffering from a stroke; Florence Harding, battling a kidney disease; and Mamie Eisenhower, enduring an inner-ear disturbance and heart problems.

INTO THE TWENTIETH CENTURY

In the twentieth century, First Ladies' social duties gradually expanded and became more visible to the public. This was a response to the increased size of the government, the extension of the right to vote to women, and finally, the development of television coverage of First Ladies' activities. Invitations to social events at the White House began to serve a variety of purposes. They were used to honor ordinary and extraordinary Americans, from members of championship sports teams, to 4-H club members, to spelling-bee winners, to Nobel Prize-winners, to successful business and labor leaders, to children with special needs, to talented artists, musicians, performers, and authors. As in the past, they also served political objectives by encouraging favorable votes in Congress, rewarding campaign contributors, and even more importantly, establishing friendlier relations between the United States and other nations.

Presidential wives received more assistance than their predecessors had. Martha Washington had help from Polly Lear, wife of her husband's chief aide, in writing and sending invitations, and other First Ladies followed her example. Edith Roosevelt, wife of President Theodore Roosevelt, however, began the practice of hiring a social secretary at government expense—not only to prepare invitations but to screen out undesirable guests who might offend Mrs. Roosevelt's high moral standards. Edith also hired caterers to prepare meals for state banquets because the White House kitchens proved inadequate once the State Dining Room was enlarged. Edith put the chief usher in charge of running the White House. This proved a boon to her successors because when social functions were scheduled, if a First Lady did not have the time or the inclination to involve herself in the details of planning, she could just approve menus suggested by the chef and delegate responsibility for flower arrangements, choice of silver, crystal, and china to the White House staff. Her social secretary could manage the seating arrangements, secure entertainers, and generally organize the festivities.

A New York aristocrat, Edith had spent time in Washington when her husband was civil service commissioner. At that time, she cultivated the friendship of leading artists and intellectuals. As First Lady, this was the group she preferred to entertain. At mass receptions for the public, she held a bouquet of flowers to avoid having to shake hands. Interestingly, one of her predecessors, Frances Cleveland, boasted that she had shaken hands with each of 5,000 guests at a reception.[12]

As the president's wife, Nellie Taft wanted to be recognized as a queenly hostess. She grew accustomed to being treated like royalty when her husband served as governor-general of the Philippines. In the White House, she planned elaborate state dinners and would even pop into the kitchen to make sure the cooks had followed her instructions for preparing terrapin (turtle) soup, one of her specialties. She was often able to talk with visiting diplomats in their own language and frequently joined the men if they tried to take her husband aside for a private conversation.

Ellen and Woodrow Wilson preferred a quiet family life to parties and social events, so they entertained as little as possible prior to Ellen's illness and death in the White House. Because of World War I and her husband's stroke, Woodrow's second wife, Edith, did not give too many dinners and receptions. Then, as America entered the Roaring Twenties and women nationwide finally gained the right to vote, First Ladies made themselves more visible as public figures. Florence Harding carefully cultivated the press so that reporters would create a favorable image of her. She even came downstairs from the family living quarters to personally guide visiting tourists through the mansion. Since the days of Florence Harding, First Ladies no longer had to pinch pennies when planning official White House social events because Congress finally passed an annual entertainment allowance for the president. Today that sum is $20,000.

Lou Hoover was a more private person than her immediate predecessors, but she and her husband rarely dined alone. Most comfortable with wealthy people like themselves, they entertained lavishly, but they had the unfortunate habit of adding guests at the last minute without informing the staff, and 500 people might show up for a party intended for 200. As a hostess, Lou had a strange affectation; she insisted upon using signals to cue the staff to serve or remove plates. These were often quite difficult to understand and led to a certain amount of confusion. A perfectionist, Lou held meetings after every party to review what had happened in order to make the next social event better.

After the formality of the Hoover years, Eleanor Roosevelt's more casual style of entertaining was suitable to the Depression era of the 1930s, when the economy collapsed and many Americans were out of work. To the astonishment of the White House staff, after her guests arrived for Sunday suppers, Eleanor would personally scramble eggs on a chafing dish to be served to them. She even offered the king and queen of England hot dogs when they were the Roosevelt's guests at the family home in Hyde Park. At official state dinners, much of the pomp and ceremony was eliminated because President Roosevelt was confined to a wheelchair and could not participate in a grand procession down the stairs.

White House servants often grew tired, but Eleanor showed no signs of fatigue as she hostessed back-to-back teas and receptions for thousands of people. In 1939, she shook hands with 14,056 people, had 4,729 in for meals, another 9,211 for teas, and had 323 house guests who stayed over at least one night.[13] In this way, she could honor the many groups and causes she supported. She would also bring in people she had just met to visit at the White House. Resident White House guests, from Prime Minister Winston Churchill of Great Britain to her husband's advisor Louis Howe, would stay for indeterminate periods, making it difficult for the staff to prepare the rooms for new arrivals. When she was on the road inspecting projects for the president, his secretary, Missy LeHand, or daughter Anna took over Eleanor's responsibilities as hostess. During World War II, formal entertainment was more limited because of security considerations and food shortages.

During the late 1940s and early 1950s, American women were idealized as homemakers and wives, not as war workers or political activists. First Ladies Bess Truman and Mamie Eisenhower fulfilled these traditional expectations by demonstrating their skills as hostesses, and American women identified with them. Bess Truman, a small-town midwesterner, had never been part of the Washington social scene during her years as a senator's wife. As a very private person, she was relieved to find her social schedule limited at first by the death of President Franklin Roosevelt and wartime conditions. Renovations of the White House further reduced the scale of formal entertaining.

Nevertheless, when called upon to be a hostess, Bess graciously officiated at formal state dinners as if she had been attending them all her life. After shaking some 4,100 hands in one week of receptions and teas, she explained that she got through it because, "I have a strong tennis arm."[14] She enjoyed herself much more, however, when her bridge club from her hometown of Independence, Missouri, arrived for a visit at the Executive Mansion. She made her share of ceremonial appearances, but some received more media coverage than others. In 1945, for example, movie newsreels captured her attempt to christen some hospital planes. To her dismay, the champagne bottles repeatedly refused to break until a naval officer smashed them with a hammer.

In 1953, when she entered the White House, Mamie Eisenhower received an average of 700 visitors a day.[15] She probably would have continued this practice throughout her eight years as First Lady if her health and that of the president had been more robust. She spent days in bed in order to have the strength to meet her social obligations. Mamie charmed the nation with her theme parties, decorating state rooms in honor of Halloween or St. Patrick's Day. Chief Usher J. B. West claimed that in planning White House social events, Mamie was "her own social director, decorator, guest-list selector, seating arranger," leaving little for her social secretary to do.[16] Because she wanted her privacy, she departed from tradition by discouraging heads of state from staying overnight at the White House and arranged for them to be accommodated at Blair House, a government-owned mansion across the street. Unlike many other First Ladies, as the wife of former Army general Dwight "Ike" D. Eisenhower, Mamie was comfortable with the requirements of protocol and precedence.

At the beginning of the sixties, East Coast socialite Jackie Kennedy used her husband's wealth to give elegant private dinner dances in the public rooms of the Executive Mansion. Growing up in a world of servants, trips to Europe, antique furnishings, opera, and ballet, theme parties were not for her. Washington society quickly abandoned cocktail parties to copy her more sophisticated style of entertaining. The First Lady turned the spotlight on the nation's most gifted and talented performing artists rather than the popular entertainers of the day. Choreographer George Balanchine, composer Leonard Bernstein, and noted cellist Pablo Casals were among her guests. The Kennedys also invited Vice President Lyndon Johnson and his wife to their private parties, something few other presidential couples had done.

Jackie cut back on the number of traditional receptions held to honor government officials. State dinners, with their tedious receiving lines, were only given for foreign dignitaries, and menus were reduced to four courses from the six Mamie had offered. To make these occasions less stuffy, fifteen round tables replaced the traditional large E-shaped banqueting table, letting conversation flow more easily. In the few large receptions they hosted, the

Jackie Kennedy brought a cosmopolitan sophistication to White House entertainment. In this photo, President Kennedy and Jackie speak with eminent cellist Pablo Casals.

Kennedys walked among their guests, creating a far more informal atmosphere. Traditionally for these events and for private parties, social secretaries had been responsible for preparing invitations, locating correct addresses for guests, instructing calligraphers (specialists in decorative handwriting) to prepare invitations and place cards for the tables, keeping track of who was coming or not, and releasing the First Lady's social schedule to the media. Under Jackie, the social secretary also served as programming director for performances given in the East Room after dinner and made sure that guests were being treated hospitably.

Jackie refused to host or attend those luncheons, teas, and ceremonial functions that normally filled a First Lady's schedule. "I can't stand those silly women," she claimed, refusing to attend a congressional wives' function.[17] The aloof and uncooperative First Lady did not wish to spend her time with politicians or their wives. She even declined to attend a Distinguished Ladies Reception intended to honor her. Officially, it was claimed that her young children needed her, although she left them behind to go off on trips abroad with her sister. When she chose to boycott an event, Jackie usually found a stand-in. On one occasion, her mother presided over a tea while the First Lady went for a walk. Another substitute who filled in for her was Lady Bird Johnson, the vice president's wife.

As the wife of a politician and as a businesswoman in her own right, Lady Bird Johnson quickly adapted to her duties as First Lady after the tragic assassination of John Kennedy in 1963. Since she and her husband both came from Texas, the White House soon became accustomed to informal Texas-size entertaining, including barbecues on the West Terrace of the building. Lady Bird and Lyndon had more than 200,000 guests during their five years in office. Under the able direction of the social secretary, a huge stage was erected in the East Room for entertainment and Broadway plays, such as *Hello Dolly,* as well as ballet troupes and Native American dancers. The Johnsons also sponsored the first performance at the Executive Mansion by a black comedian, Bill Cosby.

The Johnsons dispensed with the traditional winter reception for members of Congress and instead hosted eleven working parties so that the president, ever the consummate politician, could convince the lawmakers to pass his programs. Men and women were segregated, with Lady Bird escorting congressional wives around the Executive Mansion. As a sign of the times, she realized that some of the spouses of members of Congress were husbands, also in need of entertaining. The First Lady suggested, "Let's just let *them* decide whether or not they want to attend."[18] Some actually did and enjoyed it.

Pat Nixon became First Lady in 1969, a time when students were protesting American involvement in the Vietnam War and women's identities were no longer a reflection of their husbands' accomplishments. She was a private person forced by her husband's political career to become a public figure. Before large crowds she appeared stiff and reserved, but she could be quite warm and charming in one-on-one conversations. When the members of the Appalachian Fireside Crafts, a self-help group from the poverty-stricken mountain area, were invited to the White House to present her with a quilt, she saw how nervous they were and went around the room, giving each guest a hug.

The Nixons had even more visitors than the Johnsons. In 1970, 45,313 had been received at the White House, compared to 28,000 during the Johnsons' final year. There were 64 state and official dinners and 116 receptions.[19] More significantly, Pat shook hands with more than a quarter of a million Americans who came to tour the White House. Not since Florence Harding had a First Lady taken the time to greet them. She saw that ramps were installed to make the Executive Mansion more accessible to those in wheelchairs, arranged tours for the blind, and insisted that security guards be trained to be helpful and informative to tourists.

In August 1974, Betty Ford found herself First Lady after Richard Nixon's sudden resignation in the wake of scandal. For the next two-and-a-half years, the White House took on a happy, informal air. Betty and her husband Gerald encouraged their guests to get up on the dance floor. Having brought back Jackie Kennedy's circular tables to the State Dining Room, Betty featured American crafts as centerpieces, including Native American baskets. As a feminist, she particularly welcomed women's groups to the White House for teas and receptions.

In 1977, Rosalynn Carter and her husband Jimmy were determined to restore simplicity to social functions at the White House. As plain folks from Plains, Georgia, the former state governor and his wife eliminated much of the traditional pomp from state dinners, including the color guard and herald trumpets. Evening events were scheduled a half hour earlier to accommodate the Carters' dining habits, and parties ended earlier, too, since the Carters eliminated dancing. To save money, Rosalynn Carter chose not to serve liquor at White House festivities, although it was available in the family's private quarters. "I'm not a prude!" she insisted.[20] To their credit, the Carters brought White House entertainments into the homes of average Americans by permitting public television to tape the proceedings, which have been aired ever since as a series called "In Performance at the White House." The first program featured brilliant classical pianist Vladimir Horowitz and commentary by Jim Lehrer.

When the "Me Generation" came of age, homeless people became more numerous; yet cutting back on federal expenditures became an official policy. Using private funding, First Lady Nancy Reagan ordered a $200,000 set of china for state dinners. The purchase was announced the day before Ronald Reagan's administration offered a plan to lower nutrition standards for school lunch programs. It was no wonder that she was lambasted by the media and lampooned by television comedians. For the first time in American history, a president had to defend his wife's judgment at a press conference. The First Lady's detractors had already started calling her "Queen Nancy" after her visit to Britain for the wedding of Prince Charles and Princess Diana, where she hobnobbed so conspicuously with the royal family. The purchase of expensive china played right into their hands. Of course, it was easier to criticize the First Lady for extravagance than to find fault with her very popular husband.

Nancy decided to bring back elegance and fashion to White House entertaining. She had always admired Jackie Kennedy and sought to follow her example. A perfectionist, this former movie actress and California governor's wife personally directed the creation of flower arrangements for state dinners, sampled meals to be served in advance, and often recommended changes in the menu. She frequently served tiny portions of food artistically arranged on the plate, an expensive style called "West Coast Nouvelle." She issued invitations to the rich and famous, and they joined her at the White House for lavish parties. Her style suited the times—flashy, extravagant, and glamorous.

During the 1980s and 1990s, more and more women entered the workforce, yet Nancy Reagan and her successor, Barbara Bush, were examples of women who devoted themselves to their husbands' political careers. Like Nancy, Barbara Bush had grown accustomed to playing the role of hostess as her husband moved up the political ladder. Barbecues were her favorite style of feeding a house full of guests, not all of whom had been expected. At the White House, though, she preferred to serve buffet-style and then show a movie. The dress code was casual. Often these visitors were taken on a tour of the private living quarters, which they found fascinating. The Bushes gave many parties, more or less running a constant open house. In addition to politicians, reporters, heads of government departments, business leaders, and sports stars, there were numerous grandchildren to be fed and entertained. For state dinners, however, George and Barbara were as formal as the Reagans, and they arranged the seating plans themselves. As a hostess, Barbara's warmth could be seen in the way she hugged her guests and put an arm around them when posing for photographs.

When Hillary Rodham Clinton became First Lady in 1993, she made White House entertaining more health-conscious, reflecting the values of her baby-boomer generation. She banned smoking from the Executive Mansion and insisted that the chefs prepare healthier meals. Some of her guests found that the food was far less appetizing than that of previous administrations, but then again, they may have been expecting the creations of French chefs. Setting the tone for her role as First Lady during the next four years, Hillary stated, "I am very conscious of the social and hostess responsibilities—I did the same thing in Arkansas and actually I like it. I like being able to bring people together and entertain them and enjoy their company. But at the same time, I have the need to do something I feel is important, . . . that goes beyond the accepted duties of the First Lady."[21] She hosted a number of teas and receptions but only a few ceremonial dinners for foreign leaders. Washington society began to view the Clintons as a rather unsocial presidential couple. In 1996, the Clintons were criticized for allegedly exchanging nights in the White House for political favors or donations.

Since the earliest days of the American republic, the First Lady has been expected to serve as the nation's hostess, balancing aristocratic elegance with democratic simplicity. Whether she will continue to do so remains to be seen. During the nineteenth century, presidential wives delegated this duty to others. Perhaps in the twenty-first century, official hostesses can be designated to relieve the First Lady, if there are more important duties for her to perform. The social secretary is well equipped to handle this obligation. Over the course of the twentieth century, she has been taking over more and more of the preparations for White House social events. No matter who invites and greets White House guests, social life at the Executive Mansion will continue to flourish to the great satisfaction and fascination of ordinary citizens.

▐ ▌▐ ▌▐ ▌ THREE ▐ ▌▐ ▌▐ ▌▐ ▌

MAKING A FASHION
STATEMENT

*"I must dress in costly material.
The people scrutinize every article
that I wear with critical curiosity."*
—Mary Lincoln

First Lady Mary Lincoln was the first presidential wife to be criticized in the press for pursuing an extravagant lifestyle. She was condemned for buying new clothes while men were dying on the battlefields of the Civil War. In early 1862, she acquired sixteen dresses, which set tongues wagging and kept newspaper reporters busy describing them and denouncing her. The First Lady had been raised in Lexington, Kentucky, where dressing up was seen as a mark of elegance. For her, clothes indicated one's position and station in life.

Often a very insecure woman, Mary felt that she had to "dress for success" despite the war and the debts she ran up. "I must dress in costly material. The people scrutinize every article that I wear with critical curiosity," she told her dressmaker and friend, Elizabeth Keckly, a former slave.[1] As the wife of a president, Mary was determined to wear the latest styles and costly fabrics. When Union wives approached her to join their boycott of imported fabrics, she turned them down. She had consulted her husband and

Insecure, Mary Lincoln spent enormous amounts of money on her appearance. Still, she was rejected in Washington, D.C. social circles as an uncouth Westerner.

the secretary of the Treasury, who informed her that the government needed the money it collected by taxing these materials.

In the 1860s, dresses were made by seamstresses; they were not purchased off the rack in boutiques or department stores. For the latest styles, Mary consulted *Godey's Lady's Book*, the fashion magazine of the day. It featured sketches and descriptions of clothes created for Empress Eugenie of France, wife of Napoleon III, including gowns worn over large steel hoops, requiring as many as 25 yards of material. Mary and other fashionable American women wore these exaggerated hoop skirts with bodices that bared arms and necks, allowing them to display costly jewelry. She preferred white and bold primary colors, more suitable to young ladies than to a 43-year-old First Lady.

Mary's new fashions displeased most Western congressmen, who were accustomed to seeing their wives in more concealing clothes. Her husband, Abraham, however, liked the way she looked. Nevertheless, on one occasion, he did take exception to his wife's new low neckline and long train by saying, "Whew! Our cat has a long tail tonight—if some of that tail were nearer the head, it would be in better style."[2]

In 1864, by the time her husband was up for reelection, Mary told a friend that she had spent $27,000 on clothing, but the sum was actually higher.[3] Not only did she have gowns made, she bought numerous accessories to go with them. Lincoln only earned $25,000 a year as president and had no idea how much his wife had actually spent on her apparel. He had allowed her only a few hundred dollars to outfit herself.

She got into trouble in the first place because she had failed to realize that fabrics and trimmings for dresses cost more in Washington and New York than in Illinois, where she had lived with her husband before he became president. A compulsive shopper, Mary frequently traveled to New York on a private railroad car to go on shopping sprees. Merchants offered her unlimited credit because a First Lady's business would help their sales. They frequently gave her gifts to lure her into becoming a steady customer, but it wasn't always clear to her which items were gifts and which were purchases. For example, she accepted an imported shawl from store owner Alexander Stewart and then was surprised to be billed for the item four months later. Fifty years earlier, Dolley Madison had received gifts of clothing from merchant John Jacob Astor and was not criticized by the press. It was no wonder that Mary Lincoln was perplexed.

More importantly, Mary feared that if her husband failed to be reelected, the merchants would press him to pay her debts. Then he would find out how much she really owed. To avoid that possibility, she held off her creditors by renegotiating outstanding bills and continuing to make purchases from them. Privately, she also solicited donations from Republican politicians, arguing, "Hundreds of them are getting immensely rich off the patronage [political favors] of my husband, and it is but fair that they should help me out of my embarrassment."[4] They came to her rescue, aware that the Democrats were planning to make Mary's extravagance a campaign issue and that the president's reelection bid would be hurt if the merchants went public about the First Lady's unpaid bills. These Republicans may also have been fearful that Mary knew enough about their own political misdeeds to blackmail them if they did not help her.

Even with their contributions, she still faced a debt of about $10,000 that had to be renegotiated and settled after President Lincoln was assassinated in April 1865. That summer, in what the press called the "Old Clothes Scandal," the former First Lady tried to sell off her fabulous wardrobe. There were no buyers. She was able to return some of her jewelry to the dealer who sold it to her, and eventually her debts were refinanced into a high-interest loan.

Like Mary Lincoln, modern First Lady Nancy Reagan also became obsessed with "dressing for success" as First Lady. The adopted daughter of a wealthy, conservative doctor, she became a socialite, accustomed to an elegant lifestyle. Her friends were wealthy society matrons and Hollywood celebrities she had met when her actor-husband became president of the Screen Actors Guild, a spokesman for General Electric, and governor of California. At Ronald Reagan's inauguration as president, she got off on the wrong foot with the public by wearing American designer clothes and accessories worth approximately $25,000.[5] She had a flair for wearing clothes and was genuinely interested in high fashion, but reporters and columnists focused on the cost and the source of her spectacular wardrobe.

In the past, as was common among socialites, she had accepted free gowns from noted American designers, eager to have their creations photographed or mentioned in the society pages of the newspapers. After she wore them, Nancy usually gave the gowns to costume collections. She continued this practice as First Lady but was repeatedly criticized by reporters. She was also taken to task for wearing lavish clothes and jewels in Britain at the royal wedding in July 1981. After so much negative media coverage, a poll revealed that 62 percent of the American people believed she put "too much emphasis on style and elegance at a time of economic recession."[6]

The controversy over her free clothing refused to disappear because a First Lady was expected to set a higher standard than a socialite. If her outfits were loans, she should have returned them and not donated them. If the clothes were gifts, they should have been included in the Reagan's tax return. Furthermore, the 1977 Ethics in Government Act required the president and his wife to report all presents worth more than $35. To avoid tax and ethics problems, spokespeople at the White House announced that the First Lady's designer clothing was loaned and that she would continue to donate it to museums. A month later, when the furor failed to subside, Mrs. Reagan's press secretary issued the following statement: "The First Lady will discontinue accepting clothes from American designers, but she will continue to donate her own clothes to museums because she believes that the clothing of any particular era is a visual story of the people of that period."[7]

Although she was upset with the bad press she was receiving, Nancy mended fences with humor. In 1982, at the reporters' annual Gridiron Dinner, known for its witty and satirical entertainment, she made a surprise appearance on stage dressed as a bag lady and sang specially written lyrics to an old song from the 1920s, "Secondhand Rose." The original lyrics bemoaned the singer's need to wear used clothing. Nancy used the tune to poke fun at herself and her passion for high fashion.

Mary Lincoln and Nancy Reagan were hounded by the media because they were accused of violating political and ethical standards in pursuit of fashion. Other First Ladies' style of dressing was subject to controversy, too, but their conduct was beyond reproach. For example, some reporters criticized Lucy Hayes for wearing solemn, dark dresses; Eleanor Roosevelt for trying a new shade of lipstick and matching nail polish; Pat Nixon for always appearing impeccably groomed with not a hair out of place; Rosalynn Carter for choosing the same gown for the Inaugural Balls that she had worn when her husband became governor of Georgia; Hillary Rodham Clinton for using hair bands, paying little attention to her appearance, and then posing in very sensual clothing for *Vogue,* a fashion magazine. Is it a coincidence that most of these First Ladies were not especially fashion conscious?

The clothing of the nation's earliest presidential wives had little impact on the women of the nation. Until the mid-nineteenth century, newspapers and magazines rarely covered the First Ladies or their style of dress. Martha Washington chose to dress plainly, and the fabric for her clothing was spun and woven in her own home. She justified her personal preference with the belief that simplicity and dignity were appropriate for officials and their wives in the newly formed republic. She was not a fashion leader, but guests at her receptions competed with one another to wear the latest European styles, featuring fabrics of silk, satin, or heavy brocades, which were ornamented with lots of ruffles.

One of her successors, Dolley Madison, became the first presidential wife to start a fashion trend, at least in the nation's capital. For her own pleasure, she wore colorful turbans with long feathers that soon became her trademark. The wives of government officials quickly began to imitate her. Released from Quaker austerity, Dolley developed a passion for clothes, particularly imported French fashions. These garments featured flimsy fabrics, high waists, and low necklines, suitable for much younger women. Dolley, however, was so charming that she was able to wear them with distinction.

With the development of the telegraph and railroads, newspapers were able to report the latest events and achieve wider circulation. To attract more readers, they began to feature human-interest stories. Since more women had become literate, articles about First Ladies began to appear with some regularity, and presidents' wives truly began to influence what American women wore.[8] In the 1880s and 1890s, photographs of First Lady Frankie Cleveland led American women to slavishly imitate her hairstyles. Advertisers used her name without her permission to sell everything from soap, to ashtrays, to underwear. A bill to stop this practice failed in Congress, so she had to live with unwanted and widespread commercialization of her name.

When reporters needed material to fill their columns, they could always mention a president's wife. As a result, in the 1880s, some bored newsmen manufactured a story that started a fashion trend. They falsely claimed that Frankie had stopped wearing the bustle, a cumbersome contraption of padding worn below the waist at the back of a skirt. After the story appeared, she did not wish to appear old-fashioned, so she wore dresses without bustles, and most other American women followed her lead.

Continuing into the twentieth century, First Ladies dressed to please their husbands, to express their own personalities, or to be stylish. At the same time, they often made a fashion statement and influenced what American women wore. During the 1920s, feminine clothing styles changed radically, reflecting perhaps women's

Newspaper stories of Frankie Cleveland's hairstyles and dress changed fashion across the United States.

newfound freedom to vote and their growing sense of independence and self-worth. President Coolidge loved to buy his wife, Grace, new clothes and often accompanied her on shopping trips. With her husband's approval, she wore the new low-hipped, shorter dresses, but her hems were not as high as some of the new designs. Grace Coolidge clearly dressed to please her indulgent husband, but because of the clothes she wore and the coverage she received in the media, she determined which fashions would be popular with American women.

Both Bess Truman and Mamie Eisenhower chose their clothes to express their own personalities. Their selections offered an interesting contrast. By now, American women were even more aware of First Ladies' fashions because television brought the presidents' wives into homes across the nation. Harry Truman defended Bess's conservative gowns, matronly suits, and untinted gray hair, saying, "She looks exactly as a woman her age should look."[9] Mamie did not. While Bess set no fashion trends, many American women copied Mamie's hairstyle, featuring bangs across the forehead. She was partial to the color pink and wore the full-skirted, wasp-waisted dresses and gowns that were becoming popular with much younger women. These very feminine styles reflected a revived interest in domesticity. As their brothers, husbands, and boyfriends returned from World War II, women were no longer expected to find fulfillment in jobs. They were supposed to become contented homemakers.

During the 1960 presidential campaign, a fashion newspaper accused the elegant young socialite Jackie Kennedy of spending $45,000 on her stylish and expensive designer outfits. An angry Jackie retorted, "I couldn't do that without wearing sable underwear."[10] Her statement made the front page of the *New York*

Jackie Kennedy's beauty and sophistication also made her a ripe target for reporters claiming she spent thousands on clothing.

Times, embarrassing her husband, John, the Democratic presidential candidate. The public never knew that in 1962 she actually spent $121,000 on clothes and related items.[11] After John Kennedy was sworn in as president, women began copying Jackie's short, simple dresses, cropped suit jackets, and pillbox hats. They admired her youthful, dignified look. Her successor, Lady Bird Johnson, sponsored the first White House fashion show. By featuring handpainted scarves with American scenes, she was able to promote her husband's "Discover America" program.

During the 1992 presidential campaign, American women breathed a sigh of relief. As an antidote to Nancy Reagan's petite figure and stylish clothes, Barbara Bush arrived at the White House with her white hair, full figure, and fake pearls, the latter intended to hide the wrinkles around her neck. Like Bess Truman, she was comfortable with who she was and how she looked. Barbara refused to change her appearance to help her husband, George, get elected and commented, "My mail tells me a lot of white-haired, wrinkled ladies are tickled pink."[12] Her no-nonsense approach to dressing and self-deprecating humor about her looks drew more applause than criticism. She even made fun of herself by appearing at the Gridiron Dinner in a blonde wig.

Her successor, Hillary Rodham Clinton, did not seek to establish any fashion trends. Although her frequent changes of style were noted and sometimes criticized in the media, Hillary admitted, "I try different types of clothes, I don't take it seriously. . . . I think it's fun."[13] It remains to be seen whether future First Ladies treat fashion seriously or casually and how important their sense of style is to the media and the public.

In 1914, some of the gowns worn by presidents' wives were displayed at the Smithsonian Institution in Washington, D.C. First Lady Helen Taft made the first contribution to the collection. In 1992, the collection was reorganized as "First Ladies: Political Role and Public Image."[14] It presents First Ladies as historically important figures in their own right, not just as women living in the reflected glory of their husbands. In addition to clothing, campaign items, White House programs, and other memorabilia are showcased. While making fashion statements remains a traditional part of the First Lady's job, the Smithsonian exhibition reminds Americans that presidents' wives have performed other more important duties.

▮▮▮▮▮▮▮ FOUR ▮▮▮▮▮▮▮

HOMEMAKING AT THE WHITE HOUSE

"I am very anxious to see the family of the President provided for properly, and while I am here I hope to get the present building put into good condition."
—Caroline Harrison

Abigail Adams, the first occupant of the White House, moved into the Executive Mansion in 1800. Appalled by what she saw, she wrote, "Not one room or chamber is finished of the whole. To assist us in this great castle, and render less attendance necessary, bells are wanting [to summon servants]."[1] She complained that the main and back staircases were not completed, the house was damp and drafty, and logs were needed for the fireplaces. To make matters worse, the nearest supply of fresh water for drinking and washing was half a mile away, and servants had to fetch it. Water wouldn't be piped into the White House until 1835. Abigail also noted that there was no yard where washing could be hung to dry, which is why she had servants hang laundry in the unfinished East Room. Within two weeks, Congress furnished the funds for a workman to make the White House more livable. He also built an outdoor privy (toilet) for the First Family's use.

Abigail was certainly not the only presidential wife to find fault with the Executive Mansion. When Theodore Roosevelt unexpectedly became president upon the assassination of William McKinley in 1901, Edith "Edie" Roosevelt made plans to move her family of eight to the White House. To her great dismay, there wasn't enough space to comfortably house her six children and their pets. To make matters worse, on the second floor, only a glass screen divided the living quarters from the executive offices of the president. This meant that people wishing to see Theodore on business would be intruding on his family's privacy. "Edie says it's like living over the store," Theodore commented.[2]

With funds supplied by Congress in early 1902, Edith hired a prestigious New York architectural firm and personally supervised the reconstruction of the White House. To give the family privacy, a West Wing was added to the Executive Mansion for the offices of the president and his staff. Sweeping away the clutter of previous administrations, she had the public rooms on the first floor restored to reflect the style of the early 19th century. She had the architects add a gallery for the portraits of First Ladies and cases to display historic White House china. Finally, she had a tennis court laid out so Theodore could get more exercise. The entire project took six months.

Almost every First Lady had complaints about the Executive Mansion and sought to make changes, but some improvements were more needed than others. In 1814, the original Executive Mansion was burned and gutted by the British during the War of 1812; rebuilding and refurnishing were not completed until 1818, when the Monroes occupied the residence. Elizabeth Monroe and her husband, James, were criticized because they ordered many fine pieces of furniture and other ornate decorations from France. Their purchases offended those who preferred simpler, more republican furnishings and those who supported American manufacturers. Over the years, the decor in the public rooms was changed as sofas and chairs wore out from frequent use. When presidential wives refurbished the White House, their taste often reflected their times. The private living quarters were also redone to accommodate the needs of presidential families.

The White House as it probably appeared before it was burned in 1814.

Many First Ladies made alterations in the White House for the comfort of their families. The Executive Mansion benefited from and showcased the latest technology and appliances. In the 1850s, under the Fillmores, a kitchen stove, central heating, and a bathroom were installed. Abigail Fillmore also received money from Congress to add a library. In 1873, as part of Julia Grant's overhaul and redecoration projects, closets were built to store clothing and other items. In 1877, Rutherford and Lucy Hayes added a telegraph and telephones after they saw a demonstration by inventor Alexander Graham Bell. In 1882, Chester Arthur added an elevator.

Some First Ladies, however, had reservations about efforts to modernize the White House. In 1848, gaslight replaced White House oil lamps and candles, but skeptical First Lady Sarah Polk insisted on keeping one chandelier lit with candles. Her decision was wise because the gaslight failed the first time it was used at a reception. The rooms were plunged into darkness except for a hall illuminated by Sarah's chandelier. Yet she had no objections to the new icebox that arrived in 1849.

In 1890, Caroline Harrison was afraid to turn on the newly installed electric lights and had the servants operate them for her. Electric appliances were already used in homes as labor-saving devices, so she was following rather than setting a trend. She did welcome other construction projects in the Executive Mansion, such as the addition of private bathrooms. In a newspaper interview she explained, "I am very anxious to see the family of the President provided for properly, and while I am here I hope to get the present building put into good condition."[3] The removal of an old china closet prompted her to start the White House collection of sets of dishes, cups, and serving platters used by previous First Ladies. She even designed the china used during her husband's presidency. Since a woman's homemaking skills were more highly valued than her educational attainments, Caroline was praised for her domesticity rather than for her other activities, such as her efforts to make the Johns Hopkins Medical School admit women.

1935, First Lady Eleanor Roosevelt began a modernization project. After the dismayed First Lady toured the old-fashioned, unhygienic cooking facilities, she arranged for an all-electric, stainless-steel kitchen to be installed, including the Mansion's first automatic dishwasher. Along with Nellie Taft, Eleanor was one of the few First Ladies ever to visit the White House kitchen. Earlier, in 1933, her husband had a swimming pool constructed so he could exercise despite his paralyzed legs. (President Nixon later turned it into a press room.) In 1934, Franklin had the West Wing enlarged and added the Cabinet Room so he could have a special place to meet with the heads of government departments. An East Wing was erected in the early 1940s to provide office space for White House assistants and the First Lady's staff.

RADICAL RECONSTRUCTION

Occasionally, a president has ordered changes made in the White House to please his wife. In 1948, President Harry S. Truman had a balcony erected on the second floor of the White House to make Bess feel more comfortable in the Executive Mansion and lure her into spending more time in Washington. During her husband's presidency, she often returned to her family's home in Independence, Missouri, which featured a large outdoor porch. She did not have much time to enjoy the new balcony, however, because engineers soon discovered that the White House was on the verge of collapse. During the summer of 1948, the president's bathroom nearly fell through the ceiling into the Red Room, and his daughter's piano did break through the floor. The Commissioner of Public Buildings told a Senate Committee that "the second floor was staying up there purely from habit."[4]

Although she rarely issued public statements, Bess urged Congress to remodel the Executive Mansion instead of replacing it with a modern residence, as some were urging. Her views triumphed. The Trumans moved across the street to Blair House

In 1948, the interior structure of the White House was gutted to make way for a complete rebuilding project.

after Harry won the presidential election of 1948. The interior of the White House was carefully removed and inventoried, the contents cataloged to be restored after new walls and floors were put in. Then the mansion was entirely gutted and rebuilt at a cost of about $5.5 million.[5] Only the old outer wall of the original White House could safely be retained. Central air conditioning was added along with modern plumbing and heating while the work was in progress. Afterward, televisions were installed.

The Commission on Renovation and a New York department store supervised the decorations. "I'm only going to be around for a year. It would be unfair to the next First Lady to impose too many of my ideas upon the house," Bess explained.[6] In 1952, the Trumans returned to the structurally sound, historically restored building. Not since the burning of the White House had such major construction been undertaken to preserve and modernize the president's residence.

Since the 1950s, presidential couples have made further alterations in the White House. In 1961, Jackie Kennedy had a kitchen and private dining room constructed in the living quarters so that her children could be raised with more privacy. More important, she began a project to restore historic furniture and decorations to the White House (See Chapter 8). Lady Bird Johnson converted Grace Coolidge's sun room into a recreation room, with a soda fountain, so her two teenaged daughters would have a placé to entertain their friends. They also enjoyed the screening room the Eisenhowers had added for movie viewing.

Unlike most of her predecessors, Nancy Reagan was criticized as extravagant when she redecorated the private rooms on the second floor in 1981. She had raised over $800,000 from private funds for the project. All the public read about were gifts of $1,800 draperies and $1,200 hairdryers, but Nancy insisted that "a lot of the money went for basics like plumbing and air conditioning and restoring the marble floor downstairs. It wasn't all spent on the second floor."[7]

MANAGING THE STAFF

Making changes in the White House was not the only way First Ladies and their husbands turned the Executive Mansion into a home. Just as important was the task of managing a staff of servants to ensure that the family quarters and public rooms were presentable, that the food was palatable, and that guests were treated hospitably. Slaves worked in the Executive Mansion until the Civil War. Since they had little incentive to do their jobs well, the rooms were often dusty and dirty. In addition, the White House was staffed by paid servants and the personal maids and valets First Ladies brought with them. For the large dinner parties from 1809–1817, Dolley Madison hired extra slaves from nearby plantations at 35 cents each to ensure that all the guests had their own waiters. To save money, Sarah Polk dismissed the salaried White House servants in 1845 and filled their positions with slaves who slept in the basement. When Mary Lincoln became First Lady in 1861, slave labor was abandoned, and she personally managed the servants to ensure that the rooms measured up to her standards of cleanliness.

Although housekeeping was an important measure of a woman's value in the nineteenth and early twentieth centuries, labor-saving appliances gradually enabled women to take on more duties outside the home. They began to spend less time on the traditional chores of cooking and cleaning. For the most part, the busy presidential wives delegated housekeeping responsibilities while the less active First Ladies more closely supervised the running of the White House. First Ladies' relationships with their servants often produced some interesting stories.

In 1909, Nellie Taft hired Mrs. Elizabeth Jaffray at government expense as the first housekeeper for the Executive Mansion. Jaffray met with the First Lady to consult on menus, shop for food, and manage the twenty-seven servants who kept the Mansion running. Since the Tafts still had to pay for all food served at the White House, Nellie was determined to economize. She kept a cow on the grounds to supply the White House with fresh milk and butter. She ordered the housekeeper to buy foods wholesale and not to serve costly out-of-season dishes. On the other hand, Nellie insisted that the staff wear fancy uniforms. As the wife of the former governor of the Philippines, Nellie often complained, "They don't do things in the White House the way we used to do them at the Malacañang

From the early nineteenth century to modern times, running the White House as a household has demanded servants and someone to direct them.

Palace [the governor's official residence]."[8] Her regal airs did not endear her to the staff.

While personally kind and thoughtful to the servants, Lou Hoover's demands made the ushers, maids, and housemen think they were working at Buckingham Palace rather than the White House in the early 1930s. They were expected to be invisible and silent when the Hoovers walked down a corridor or entered a room. Bells would sound, and the help would have to get out of sight, often hiding themselves in a closet, similar to the game of sardines. Lou also required proper formal service in the dining room, and if a butler (waiter) made the slightest error, he would find himself transferred to other duties.

Her successor, Eleanor Roosevelt, created a more relaxed atmosphere in the White House by ending the "game of sardines." She even encouraged servants to ride along in the elevator with her, something the Hoovers would not tolerate. Her attitude toward housekeeping reflected her busy life and many political and social commitments. She delegated responsibility to the servants and expected them to carry out her orders promptly because she didn't have time to repeat or clarify her requests. She often forgot an instruction as soon as she gave it. Problems arose because her notes to the staff were often illegible and she hardly had time to notice errors in service. As a result, the White House began to look shabby. This drew complaints.

One citizen wrote to Eleanor, "Instead of tearing around the country, I think you should stay at home and personally see that the White House is clean."[9] This was actually Mrs. Henrietta Nesbitt's responsibility. Eleanor had hired her as housekeeper, but she was not up to overseeing twenty-six servants charged with the maintenance of 60 rooms, 20 baths, and 160 windows. Nor did she plan interesting meals for the Roosevelt family. To the president's disgust, she served the same simple, overcooked foods day in and day out. She remained on the job because Roosevelt hated to fire employees and Eleanor would not do it for him.

Bess Truman locked horns with Mrs. Nesbitt soon after she moved into the White House in 1945. Although her husband detested brussel sprouts, the housekeeper served them nightly. Then she refused to give Bess a stick of butter to bring to her bridge club, citing wartime rationing (limiting the food supply by issuing stamps for scarce items). When the chief usher heard the story, he agreed to replace Mrs. Nesbitt. Having kept house herself, Bess constantly reminded the maids to remove dust from the bedrooms and wipe off fingerprints. Yet she was thoughtful of their needs and sent them home on Sunday afternoons, claiming, "I can turn down the beds perfectly well by myself."[10] The Trumans departed from custom by introducing the servants to their guests. It was no wonder they were popular among the domestic staff.

Mamie Eisenhower, like Bess, focused her attention on the smooth running of the White House. Although she never learned to prepare food herself, she encouraged the cook in the Executive Mansion to try every new product she read about in the papers, including the latest cake mixes. Mamie cared about the servants and constantly showed her interest in their personal lives with thoughtful acts, like sending them flowers when they were ill. She was, however, a very demanding person, issuing reams of orders through the housekeeper. Footprints on carpets especially bothered her, and she was constantly reminding the staff to vacuum them away. She also insisted that food be purchased cheaply and not be wasted. The Eisenhowers willingly ate leftovers.

As First Lady, Jacqueline Kennedy did not hold regular conferences with the domestic staff as Bess and Mamie had. She dropped in on the chief usher at random times with her ideas for a dinner, the placement of a piece of furniture, flower arrangements, or staff reassignments. Her main concern was the servants' performance on the job, and she flooded the chief usher with detailed handwritten memos about her evaluation of their work and her expectations of what they should do. Concerned with their privacy, the Kennedys made each member of the staff sign a pledge not to write anything about their work for the family, but the pledges had no legal force. When Lady Bird Johnson suddenly found herself replacing Jackie, she told the chief usher to continue to manage the White House, explaining, "I've been running a house for thirty years, I want to devote my time to other things."[11] Many of her successors would follow her example.

Sometimes, First Ladies deliberately took action as homemakers to set an example for the nation. During World War I, Woodrow Wilson's second wife, Edith, publicized her observance of meatless days to encourage Americans to do without beef and poultry so that more food could be diverted to the armed services, a practice Eleanor Roosevelt followed as well. Edith also let sheep graze on the White House lawn to keep it trim and conserve manpower. She auctioned off their wool to aid the war effort. In the 1960s, Jackie Kennedy purchased White House glassware from West Virginia to draw attention to the fine craftsmanship in poverty-stricken Appalachia. In the 1970s, Rosalynn Carter and her husband wore sweaters to ward off chills after turning down thermostats in the Executive Mansion in order to convince the public to use less energy and make the nation less dependent on foreign oil.

For the most part, however, First Ladies' influence has been more subtle. As the times demanded, they have demonstrated their household skills and domesticity by taking an active interest in the running of the White House. They have transformed the Executive Mansion into a home for their families as well as a symbol of national splendor and have equipped it with the latest conveniences while preserving its traditions. At other times, First Ladies have also shown American women that their value need not depend on their domestic skills. They have delegated responsibility for the daily operation of the mansion to others so that they could devote themselves to other interests.

▮▮▮▮▮▮▮▮ FIVE ▮▮▮▮▮▮▮

PROMOTING
FAMILY VALUES

*"If you bungle raising your children,
I don't think whatever else you
do well matters very much."*
—Jackie Kennedy

In January 1977, four days after her parents moved into the White House, nine-year-old Amy Carter attended her first classes at a Washington, D.C., public school. Her mother Rosalynn wrote, "There was a lot of press interest because we had decided that she would go to a public rather than a private school. Jimmy [President Carter] had struggled with the problem of good students leaving the public schools when he had served on the School Board all those years at home, and we didn't want to be part of the problem now."[1] Ever since the Supreme Court's 1954 decision ending racial segregation in public schools, white families had been moving to the suburbs, leaving inner-city public schools racially imbalanced. Such was also the case in Washington, D.C., where most of the permanent residents were African-Americans. As concerned Southerners from Plains, Georgia, the Carters were committed to quality education in public schools for children of all races.

On her first day of school, Amy was accompanied by her mother and secret service agents. As they got out of the car, the First Lady and her daughter were greeted by photographers' flashbulbs and queries from reporters. Amy simply smiled and entered the building without answering questions, as she had long since learned to do. Her classmates quickly accepted the presence of secret service agents, but other children in the school still regarded Amy as an object of curiosity when she went out to the playground. During the first week, there was so much confusion that her teacher kept her indoors with the agents while the rest of the class went out to play. Understandably she was quite unhappy because she did not like to be treated differently from the other children. It did not happen again. The school had children from 28 different countries, and Amy soon made friends with many of them, bringing them home to the White House to stay overnight.

Wherever she went, Amy Carter became
the object of intense scrutiny.

The Clintons, like the Carters, were equally committed to racially integrated schools and high educational standards for American children. Nevertheless, when the former governor of Arkansas and his wife entered the White House in January 1993, they chose to send their only child, Chelsea, to the Sidwell Friends School, a private institution. Their decision stirred a furor in the media, but Hillary stood her ground, because Sidwell was accustomed to handling the children of VIPs and would readily cooperate with secret service requirements for Chelsea's security. The First Lady and her husband "did not want to disrupt the lives of several hundred public school kids merely to make a symbolic statement about their support for public education."[2] Like Amy, 13-year-old Chelsea brought her school chums home to the White House for visits.

The Carters' and Clintons' choices for their daughters' schooling reflected different parenting styles even more than political considerations. Amy participated in many White House activities and was even permitted to attend state dinners, during which she often read a book to stave off boredom. Chelsea Clinton, on the other hand, did not attend one of these formal occasions until she was sixteen. Hillary Clinton had decided that her daughter should be sheltered as a preteen, but when she grew older, she appeared more frequently in public, accompanying her mother on official foreign trips and campaigning with her parents for her father's reelection. Despite their contrasting approaches to rearing a child in the White House, both First Ladies wanted their daughters to lead a somewhat normal life in the Executive Mansion.

GROWING UP IN THE WHITE HOUSE

Many of their predecessors shared these concerns, and above all, they wanted to raise their children as much as possible in privacy. In 1869, Julia Grant asked her husband to have the White House gates closed to prevent reporters and curiosity seekers from strolling the grounds and annoying her two youngest children. "Nellie [age 14] and Jess [age 11] had no place to play."[3] She got her wish.

Frankie Cleveland also tried to protect her children while giving them a normal life. Her personal popularity and the growth of mass-circulation newspapers made this increasingly difficult. In 1893, Frankie gave birth to Esther, the first child born in the White House. The candy bar Baby Ruth was named for another daughter, born in 1891. Eventually, there were three more children. The Clevelands lived in a home in the Washington, D.C. suburbs and only stayed at the White House during the social season, but they still had difficulty keeping their children's lives private. From her White House window, Frankie saw that her baby's nurse could not stop tourists from admiring Ruth out on the lawn, and once, a woman even tried to cut off one of Ruth's curls. Like Julia Grant, the First Lady ordered the White House grounds closed to the public. Unfortunately, this sparked rumors that the young Clevelands were deformed or retarded.

Aware of the difficulties Frankie had faced, Edith Roosevelt had her social secretary hand out carefully posed photographs of her children to reporters, although the accompanying text always featured her husband Theodore. She entered the White House with six children ranging in age from seventeen to three. They proved to be a handful. In this respect they were no different from other presi-

Julia Grant demanded that the White House gates be shut to protect the privacy of her two youngest children.

dential children, like Crete Garfield's son Irvin, who coasted down the grand staircase on his bicycle and ended up in the East Room.

Edith was a permissive mother who acknowledged that "Not one of my children ever wants to be told or directed about anything whatever!"[4] She relied on Theodore to discipline them. He rarely had the time. In 1903, Quentin Roosevelt was the chief troublemaker. He brought a pony into his brother Archie's White House bedroom to cheer him up when he was ill. Quentin also formed "the White House gang," a group of mischievous boys. One day, they perched on an overhead skylight and made fun of an Italian diplomat lunching with Edith. He was astonished to see them jabbering nonsense in an effort to imitate the Italian language. Another time, when reporters asked Quentin for information about his father, he replied, with a straight face, "I see him sometimes, but I know nothing about his family life."[5]

About sixty years later, Jackie Kennedy confronted the problem of raising children in the White House. To Jackie's chagrin, her husband John wanted the children photographed as a public relations ploy, but she wanted to shield them from publicity. Like the Clevelands, the Kennedys bought another home to escape from the White House. They also traveled to the family compound in Hyannisport, Massachusetts, for privacy, but photographers followed them everywhere.

"If you bungle raising your children, I don't think whatever else you do well matters very much," Jackie said.[6] Like Edith Roosevelt, she constantly read to her children. Unlike Frankie Cleveland who took her children to a kindergarten at the German Embassy, Jackie organized a nursery school for Caroline and John at the Executive Mansion so they could meet children their own age. She made her support for school integration public when she personally welcomed the son of black assistant press secretary Andrew Hatcher to the White House school. She reserved time every day to play with her children and teach them French.

Teenaged children presented special problems for First Ladies. Adolescents can be more independent and defiant than younger children. Unlike her parents, Alice Roosevelt, Theodore's daughter from a previous marriage, enjoyed all the press coverage she received and constantly sought to create a sensation by defying the social rules of the era. For example, she smoked in public, drove a car without a chaperone, and bet at racetracks. The hit song of the day, "Alice Blue Gown," was named for her and her favorite color. Neither parent was able to control this headstrong teenager.

More recent First Ladies also had to cope with teenage daughters and their social lives. Among them was Lady Bird Johnson, who often reminded 19-year-old Lynda and 16-year-old Luci to take sweaters with them when they went out on dates. Once the family was installed in the White House in 1963, she had to add, "And Luci, Lynda—don't forget to take your [Secret Service] agents along."[7] The press commented when Lynda dated movie star George Hamilton and experimented with new hair styles and makeup. Nor did reporters ignore her livelier sister Luci's conversion to Roman Catholicism before her wedding to Patrick Nugent in 1966. Lynda married Charles S. Robb a year later. In addition to Lady Bird Johnson, Elizabeth Monroe, Louisa Adams, Letitia Tyler, Julia Grant, Edith Roosevelt, Ellen Wilson, and Pat Nixon gave their children White House weddings.

Along with the joys of parenthood came the sorrows. Despite their parents' good intentions, not every presidential child had kind words to say about the way he or she was raised. Elliott

Despite the example of the Reagan children, most First Ladies and their children had open, warm relationships. Here, Betty Ford and her daughter enjoy a moment together.

Roosevelt and Patti and Michael Reagan were very critical of their parents, complaining of neglect. Fortunately, they were the exception rather than the rule.

Even more painful to First Ladies and their husbands was the death of a child. Jane Pierce, a devoutly religious woman, had lost one child in infancy and another at age four. In 1853, just two months before her husband Franklin Pierce was to be sworn in as president, her third son, eleven-year-old Bennie, was killed in a railway accident which she and Franklin survived. As First Lady, Jane secluded herself while writing letters to her late son, telling him she regretted not paying more attention to him while he was alive.

In 1862, Mary Todd Lincoln lost her middle son, eleven-year-old Willie, to typhoid fever, probably as a result of drinking polluted water from the Potomac River. Mary had two surviving sons, an older son, Robert, and a younger boy, Tad, but Willie was her favorite. "I always found my hopes concentrating on so good a boy as he," she wrote a few months after his death.[8] As was typical of her times, she did not attend Willie's White House funeral in the White House or his burial. She took to her bed for three weeks and then destroyed all signs of her dead child, sending his toys and clothes off to relatives.

On July 7, 1924, 16-year-old Calvin Coolidge, Jr., died of blood poisoning. The younger of Grace Coolidge's two sons, he had been playing tennis in sneakers without socks and had developed a blister on his foot that became seriously infected. Despite the best medical care his parents could summon, he succumbed because life-saving antibiotic drugs had not yet been discovered. Times had changed and Grace joined her husband and older son John at the funeral and burial.

She wrote to a friend, ten days after the ordeal, "We are all of us well and keeping a stiff front, trying to be as brave and courageous as Calvin was."[9] While she was no longer bubbly and laughing in public, she went on with her duties, wearing white rather than black. While her husband began his presidential campaign, she planted a spruce tree on the White House grounds in memory of her son and spent time knitting in the garden. She answered some of the many expressions of sympathy that arrived at the Executive Mansion. She was especially touched when she was given a letter that Calvin, Jr., had written to a boy his own age. "I think you are mistaken in calling me the first boy of the land, since I have done nothing. It is my father who is President. Rather, the first boy of the land would be some boy who distinguished himself through his own actions."[10] Five years later, she wrote a poem about her loss that was published in a leading women's magazine of the day.

Patrick Bouvier Kennedy, six weeks premature, was born on August 7, 1963, the first child born to a sitting president and his wife since the Cleveland's daughter Esther. Two days later, the infant died as a result of weak lungs. When President Kennedy came to the hospital to take his wife home, reporters covering the young couple noted a rare public demonstration of affection between them. They had kept their feelings for each other private, but after this tragedy, onlookers could see them drawing closer.

First Ladies often presided over intergenerational families that included parents and grandchildren in the nineteenth century. In the twentieth century, Sara Delano Roosevelt, Franklin's domineering mother, frequently stayed at the White House. She had always disapproved of Eleanor and tried to run her son and daughter-in-law's life. One member of the staff wrote, "We admired Mrs. 'R' for being able to cope with a mother-in-law who didn't mind acting more like a First Lady than the First Lady did herself."[11] Bess Truman's mother, Madge Wallace, lived with the Trumans at the White House until her death in 1952. She had been widowed for a long time and was totally dependent on Bess for companionship and guidance. Madge did not approve of Bess's husband because she considered Harry her social inferior. Although he always treated her with great politeness, she did not change her mind about him— even when he became president. On the other hand, Mamie Eisenhower's mother, Elivera Doud, got along well with her son-in-law Dwight when she lived at the White House with the presidential couple. Mamie enjoyed having her mother and other relations around but insisted that any requests they made of the White House staff be cleared through her so that they did not appear to take advantage of her position as First Lady.

Although mothers and mothers-in-law could be difficult guests, First Ladies' siblings sometimes proved to be more troublesome. Many members of Mary Lincoln's large family fought for the Confederacy during the Civil War, giving rise to false rumors that she was a traitor to the Union. She stirred up controversy when her widowed half sister came to live with her in the White House after her husband was killed fighting for the South. In 1898, when Ida

McKinley's womanizing brother George was murdered by his former lover, an Ohio seamstress, the First Lady was confronted with a sensational scandal that made headlines in all the newspapers. Although she was an invalid, she calmly attended the funeral services. Afterward, Ida acted as if the tragedy had never happened by attending a White House dinner and traveling with her husband. She didn't even wear mourning clothes. In 1994, Hillary Rodham Clinton's brother Hugh caused her embarrassment by appearing to take advantage of their relationship to launch his own political career. He ignored her advice and decided to challenge the popular Republican Connie Mack for his seat in the United States Senate. Forty-year-old Hugh was politically inexperienced and publicly admitted that he had never even voted before 1992. Hillary didn't come to Florida to campaign for him until he won the Democratic primary, an election to determine a party's official candidate for office, on his own. Despite her help, he lost the general election.

Grandchildren were a constant source of pleasure to presidential wives. First Ladies from Martha Washington to Barbara Bush were delighted when their grandchildren stayed with them. Martha Washington's son by a previous marriage, Jacky Custis, had died during the Revolutionary War, and she forced her impoverished daughter-in-law to let her adopt two of the five grandchildren, Nellie and "Little Wash." As a new First Lady, Martha wrote to a friend, "I have two of my grandchildren with me, who enjoy advantages, in point of education, and who, I trust, will be a great blessing to me."[12] In the private moments she arranged for herself, she took her grandchildren to museums, waxworks, and ventriloquist shows.

During World War II, Eleanor Roosevelt's daughter Anna and her two children, Anna Eleanor "Sisty" Dall and Curtis "Buzz" Dall, took up residence in the White House to the presidential couple's great pleasure. Son Jimmy often brought his daughter, Sarah, to visit. To keep the grandchildren happy, there was a nursery on the third floor and a sandbox and jungle gym on the South Lawn. Mamie Eisenhower's four grandchildren—David, Barbara Anne, Susan, and Mary Jean—gave her much joy. She kept an ample supply of toys for their visits and allowed them to ride their tricycles in the ground-floor corridor and swim in the pool. No nannies supervised them at the White House, but they behaved themselves. They knew their grandmother insisted on good manners. "Every moment I spend with my grandchildren is the best moment of my life," Mamie said.[13]

Grandmotherly Barbara Bush not only looked the part but lived it. By 1992, the Bushes had twelve grandchildren, who occasionally campaigned with them and often spent time with them at the Executive Mansion and at the Bush's home in Kennebunkport, Maine. Fortunately, Barbara was comfortable entertaining large numbers of people, so visits from twelve grandchildren did not faze her. She reveled in the children's rough-and-tumble antics outdoors in Maine, and as long as they were polite to visiting officials and diplomats, she had no complaints. In Washington, she took some of them out to the ballet and other events at the Kennedy Center, accompanied by her daughters-in-law. She looked forward to the annual Christmas plays the children put on for the family. As her husband left office, she wondered "if our grandchildren will remember that they danced at the White House on their grandparents' 48th Anniversary with the Marine Band playing for them?"[14]

DANGEROUS LIASONS

It was difficult for First Ladies to serve as a symbol of American family values when their husbands were unfaithful to them, but somehow they managed. Grover Cleveland had already admitted the possible paternity of an illegitimate son during his successful bid for the presidency in 1886—before he married Frankie, who knew and accepted it. In 1912, Ellen Wilson contributed to her husband's victory by allowing herself to be seen with Mary Peck, a woman who had kept the steamy letters she received from Woodrow since 1907, when they had had an affair. Having expressed her hurt and having warned her husband about the consequences of his behavior, Ellen presented Mary to the public as a family friend and even invited her to the White House to prevent harmful gossip.

Although Washingtonians heard rumors at the time, the public did not learn about most presidential affairs until after the presidents involved had died. Thus Nan Britton published a book in 1927 accusing Warren Harding of fathering her child, after he had been dead for a year. Florence had known that her husband was unfaithful. She was also aware that after Warren was nomi-

General Dwight Eisenhower (second from right) was rumored to be having an affair with his driver, Kay Summersby Morgan (right).

nated the Republican Party had paid Carrie Phillips $20,000 to stay away until after the election. Carrie was a family friend who had been involved with Warren for years.

Long before Franklin Roosevelt became president, a devastated Eleanor discovered that he was having an affair with her social secretary, Lucy Mercer. The Roosevelts agreed to stay married, but they lived separate lives. As president, Franklin sought the companionship of a number of women, although he and his wife still had bonds of affection and respect. She discreetly looked for love outside her marriage as well. Lucy Mercer Rutherfurd was with him when he died at Warm Springs on April 12, 1945.

After Dwight Eisenhower's death in 1969, his wartime driver Kay Summersby Morgan wrote a book about their relationship, published in 1976. Rumors had long been circulating about their affair, but in a 1979 interview, Mamie explicitly denied it. Jackie Kennedy took frequent trips away from the White House, often with her sister, perhaps in retaliation for her husband John's numerous affairs. She never commented on them in public, even after Judith Campbell Exner's sensationalist 1977 revelations of her ties to a mobster as well as to President Kennedy. A year after her husband died, Lady Bird Johnson responded to a question on a television interview about how she handled her late husband's womanizing. She replied, "I hope I was reasonable."[15]

The past came full circle during the 1992 presidential campaign, when reporters questioned Hillary Rodham Clinton about her husband's extramarital affairs. Confronted with a delicate situation while her husband was alive, and well aware that her responses might cost him the election, she refused to sit silently beside him during a television interview. Using her legal training, she neither confirmed nor denied the affairs but emphasized instead Bill's and her own commitment to their marriage. In the 1980s, when he was straying, she had insisted that they both receive counseling.

In the late 1990s, Bill's relationships with women surfaced again and threatened to bring down his presidency. Several women accused him of sexual harassment and he was also sued in court for damages. Hillary made a series of appearances on nationwide television to defend him, and they frequently allowed themselves to photographed as an affectionate couple.

Despite their husbands' infidelity, their children's shortcomings, difficult parents or in-laws, and demanding relatives, First Ladies have continued to personify family values. They have raised their children while coping with prying reporters, public pressure, and painful losses. Whether they were activist First Ladies or quiet models of domesticity, they have shown the American public the joys and sorrows of family life.

SIX

CARING FOR THE PRESIDENT IN SICKNESS AND IN HEALTH

"After 1955, whenever Ike gave a speech, I always sat there in utter dread that he would have a heart attack on the air."
—Mamie Eisenhower

On September 26, 1919, President Woodrow Wilson collapsed during a grueling speaking tour. He was crossing the nation, trying to convince the public to accept the treaty ending World War I and to approve American membership in the League of Nations, the world's first major international organization intended to prevent war. As the train rushed the stricken president back to the capital, reporters were told that he had suffered a nervous breakdown as a result of overwork. Back in the White House, on October 2, Wilson suffered a stroke, leaving the left side of his body paralyzed. While his second wife, Edith, went to call his doctor and close personal friend, Dr. Cary T. Grayson, the president fell unconscious on the bathroom floor. That night, Dr. Grayson issued a medical bulletin stating that "The president is a very sick man."[1] None of his subsequent bulletins was much more informative. They did little to quell rumors that the president was gravely ill. Only the president's personal secretary and the secretaries of state, the navy, and the treasury were told the truth.

Grayson summoned nurses and five medical specialists to the White House. Among them was a neurologist, Dr. Francis X. Dercum of Philadelphia. Wilson could only be declared disabled under the vague clauses of the Constitution. This his doctors refused to do. When Edith asked Dr. Dercum whether her husband ought to resign to avoid stress, he replied that "if he resigns, the greatest incentive for recovery is gone; and as his mind is clear as crystal he can still do more even with a maimed body than any one else."[2] By following Dercum's advice, Edith, in effect, began to govern the nation. She described her role more modestly:

> So began my stewardship. I studied every paper, sent from the different secretaries or senator, and tried to digest and present in tabloid form the things that, despite my vigilance, had to go to the president. I, myself, never made a single decision regarding the disposition of public affairs. The only decision that was mine was what was important and what was not, and the *very* important decision of when to present matters to my husband.[3]

Nowhere in the Constitution was the president's wife empowered to determine which matters should receive her husband's attention or to conduct interviews with government officials on her own or to decide which heads of government departments should be replaced. No First Lady before or since held so much power, albeit unofficially. There was some doubt as to whether the president even knew what was going on.

There was a power vacuum. Because he did not want to appear to be usurping the presidency, Wilson's vice president, Thomas R. Marshall, refused to become acting president without specific authorization from Congress and the approval of Dr. Grayson and Edith. This he did not get. Instead, he took over the ceremonial and social duties of the presidency while Edith remained at her stricken husband's bedside. To provide some leadership, Secretary of State Robert Lansing started holding a series of cabinet meetings, twenty in all, but the business of government was more or less suspended. Many bills passed by default without the president's signature, as the Constitution provides; government vacancies were not filled; and

After Woodrow Wilson (left) collapsed from the strain of his work, his wife, Edith (right), took over the reins of power.

foreign diplomats did not submit their credentials to the president.

The president demanded Lansing's resignation in February 1920, probably at Edith's prompting since it was known that she disliked the secretary. On April 30, 1920, Wilson held his first cabinet meeting and gradually resumed his duties, but he remained a sick and weak man. The public never found out how ill their president was until February 1920, when a newspaper released an interview with a specialist who had treated the president for another problem on October 14, 1919. The Senate failed to approve Wilson's treaty and the United States never joined the League of Nations.

If Edith Wilson can be faulted for doing too much, another First Lady can be criticized for doing too little. Eleanor Roosevelt may even have worsened her husband's condition during his illnesses in 1944–1945. She had stood by him when he developed polio in 1921 and had helped him to lead an active life despite paralysis. Along with obliging reporters and photographers, she had helped conceal from the public the fact that he could not walk independently and was confined to a wheelchair. Yet, she could not tolerate illness in herself or anyone else and detached herself from her husband's numerous ailments over the twelve years of his presidency.

In March 1944, when the president was taking too long to recover from a bout of flu and a bad cough, his daughter Anna insisted that he have a checkup at Bethesda Naval Hospital. Franklin had been sick before and regained his health, so Eleanor had refused to admit that this time was any different. She thought that his problems were mostly psychological and that he was fatigued from overwork. Her attitude was not as callous as it might seem because Franklin had good days and bad days, and even at his sickest, he could surprise everyone by rallying round as if nothing were wrong with him.

After the checkup, Franklin did not ask any questions about his health, and no information was given to him. His doctors never told Eleanor or Anna that he had congestive heart disease. He was given medication, put on a low-fat diet, and asked to reduce his intake of alcohol and cigarettes. One of his doctors wrote that Eleanor "couldn't accept that he was really sick or that he needed to cut down his activities, especially if they related to her concerns. I would sit with the family telling everyone how important it was not to annoy him or upset him at the dinner table, but she could not stop herself."[4]

Even if she had been told the nature of his illness and fully cooperated with the doctor's suggestions, it might not have prolonged her husband's life. Just before his death from a brain hemorrhage in April 1945, Eleanor wrote to a friend, "I think he faced the fact, five years ago, that if he had to go on in office to accomplish his work, it must shorten his life, and he made that choice. If he can accomplish what he set out to do, and then dies, it will have been worth it. I agree with him."[5] This time a First Lady did not act, and both she and the public remained ignorant of her husband's actual condition—even though all those around him witnessed his physical deterioration during the last months of his life.

The problem of presidential illness and disability had begun during the first administration in American history. Martha Washington discreetly took charge when doctors removed a tumor from her husband in 1789 and roped off their home from passersby and noisy carriages. In the middle of the War of 1812, when President James Madison and his assistant, Ned Coles, fell seriously ill, Dolley Madison filled in for them. She told a Senate committee that her husband couldn't see them until he felt better. The Washingtons started the tradition that a sick president was still the nation's leader, and Dolley Madison upheld it. Was this a mistake? What would happen when a president became too sick to run the country? The Constitution was not very clear about the procedures to be followed.

In the absence of clear guidelines, President Grover Cleveland and his wife Frankie decided to keep his illness a secret from the government and the public. In July 1893, he had an operation to remove a cancerous growth from the roof of his mouth. The surgery was performed on board a yacht in Long Island Sound and he recuperated at the family's summer home on Buzzards Bay in Massachusetts. Because news of his illness could have caused a financial crisis in the nation, it was kept secret. He had already summoned a special session of Congress to deal with the country's shaky economy.

His wife Frankie was one of the very few people to know what was going on. The vice president was not informed because he and the president differed over economic policy. Frankie fielded reporters' questions about her husband's absence and wrote letters for him which did not reveal that he was ill. At Buzzards Bay, she told everyone who asked that he was worn out. Tongue-in-cheek, she announced, "If the country hadn't been so inconsiderate as to get up this financial trouble, which necessitated the early session of Congress, and he could get another month here away from worry, I think he would be thoroughly rested."[6] Privately, she termed the surgery "a narrow escape."[7]

While the surgery was revealed in a newspaper article the next month, it was disclaimed as untrue since the president gave every sign of being healthy and there was no evidence that he had undergone the ordeal. (In fact, while he recuperated at Buzzards Bay, he was fitted with an artificial jaw so he could speak intelligibly, and since all the work had been done inside his mouth, there were no scars.) The story wasn't confirmed for another 24 years when one of the surgeons wrote an account of the operation for a popular magazine.

In 1967, the 25th Amendment provided a remedy for presidential disability. It permitted the president to transfer power to his vice president in the event of a serious illness. Alternatively, the vice president and the cabinet, the heads of government departments and other important government officials, could declare the president disabled in a letter to Congress. It would only provide an orderly transfer of power, however, if it was used. On March 31, 1981, after President Ronald Reagan was shot by a would-be assassin, his closest aides decided not to use the amendment, even though the president was in fact disabled. They prepared to carry on the government in his absence with the help of the vice president, who kept a low profile. The president's wife did not object.

Nancy Reagan rushed from the White House to her husband's side and granted permission for surgery to repair her husband's damaged left lung. The First Lady questioned the surgeons thoroughly about her husband's medical condition after the operation and for days afterward. So as not to further alarm the public, she told reporters that he was doing better than he actually was and gave them light-hearted stories of his progress. She also released a photo showing her with her husband in the hospital but had a nurse airbrushed out of it. After this episode she hired an astrologer to select the most favorable dates and times for him to schedule events.

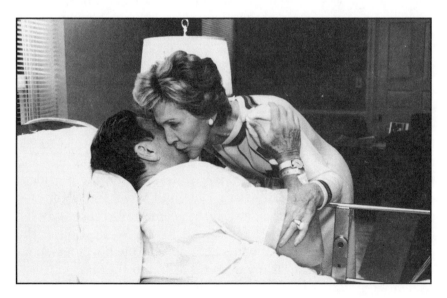

Nancy was extremely protective of her husband during his stays in the hospital.

In July 1985, doctors at Bethesda Naval Hospital discovered that President Reagan had a cancerous growth in his colon. Nancy encouraged her husband to have the corrective operation, but she did not tell him he had cancer. He did not question her or his doctors because he simply relied on her judgment and her willingness to get the necessary medical details. To avoid upsetting the stock market, Nancy stayed at the White House, where she received news that the surgery went well and that there were no further signs of the disease. A press release said very little and did not mention cancer.

This time, the Twenty-fifth Amendment was quietly invoked, and George Bush was made acting president. The vice president was told to clear with the First Lady what she wanted him to do. Nancy took over the president's ceremonial functions while he recovered, telling a Boy Scout Jamboree, for example, "I'm pinch-hitting for my favorite scout."[8] With Bush present, Nancy even read a speech prepared to be delivered by her husband at a reception.

A breathing tube was blocked by the First Lady as she bent over her husband in a photo released to the media. The president could only mumble, and what he said was intelligible only to his wife. Nancy controlled all access to her husband in concert with Chief of Staff Donald Regan, who advised the president and determined who could see him. Yet, Nancy worried that Regan was getting too much media attention and it would hurt the president's image (see Chapter Ten).

She would not allow the vice president or the chief of the National Security Council (NSC), responsible for investigating and evaluating overseas threats to the United States, to see him about an urgent matter. They were told to consult her, and when they persisted in demanding the meeting, she told them to put the problem in writing. Later in the week, she permitted the NSC chief to see the president to discuss the hostage crisis in the Middle East and suggest a way to improve relations with Iran. Later, the president would not be able to recall whether he authorized a deal to trade arms with Iran for hostages, a deal that came to be known as the Iran-Contra scandal. After he returned to the White House, the president paid tribute to his wife's activities during his illness, concluding, "Nancy Reagan is my everything,"[9] and she was.

Only ten days after the surgery, Ronald Reagan had a cancerous growth removed from his nose, the probable result of years spent in the sun. Nancy insisted that the procedure be kept from the public as well as the president. Four days later the president was told about the malignancy. The press secretary threatened to resign if he could not level with reporters, but the First Lady maintained that people would jump to the wrong conclusions. An innocuous statement was issued without the press secretary's signature, but the president himself gave the story away when he told reporters quite casually what had happened. They pounced on the press secretary for withholding information from them, but he told them to figure out why. Nancy assumed full control of the president's schedule and kept her husband virtually isolated from his aides during their summer vacation.

President Reagan's dramatic surgery was certainly not the only occasion when a president was seriously ill. What makes it particularly important is that the First Lady conspired to keep important information from the public. The motive was not sinister, but the decisions remain questionable. Do First Ladies owe their husbands the right to privacy that any patient deserves, or do they owe the nation important information about the presidents' medical condition because their husbands are also leaders of the nation? As the wives of presidents, and not as elected or appointed government officials, do they have the right to make decisions affecting the nation? Historians can only speculate what the impact might have been if the nation had been told the truth from the beginning.

GOING PUBLIC

Fortunately, not every president and First Lady intentionally kept medical information from the public. Dwight "Ike" Eisenhower provides one such example. During his three major illnesses in the 1950s, President Eisenhower, believing that President Wilson's illness was mishandled, insisted that the public be told the truth about his failing health. His wife Mamie concurred.

Ike had a heart attack in late September 1955 while on vacation in Denver, Colorado. Mamie acted promptly and phoned the doctor about her husband's chest pains. Later, when he was transported to the hospital, she stayed in an adjoining room, phoning the White House regularly to report on her husband's condition and to check that the staff were doing their jobs. She refused to believe that her husband would not recover, and her optimism cheered him. She also found time to personally sign letters acknowledging the more than eleven thousand get-well cards Ike received, and she read some of them to the president. Years later she admitted, "After

1955, whenever Ike gave a speech, I always sat there in utter dread that he would have a heart attack on the air."[10]

After his first week in the hospital, he began receiving official visitors.[11] His chief of staff, Sherman Adams, flew back and forth between Washington and Denver, briefing him and conveying his wishes to the cabinet and White House staff. Vice President Nixon conducted the cabinet meetings, signed some nonlegal, ceremonial documents, and made sure that the government ran smoothly. The president conducted a cabinet meeting for the first time in late November.

In June 1956, less than nine months after his heart attack, Ike suffered an inflamed small intestine and was operated on to remove an obstruction. Mamie moved into the hospital with him again and supervised his schedule and diet. He quickly took up his presidential duties in the hospital. In November 1957, when he suffered a stroke, she refused to allow him to host a state dinner and arranged for the vice president to see to the guests. Ike was up the next day and did some work, but from then on, Mamie called his appointment's secretary to ensure that his schedule was not too tiring and monitored his health even more closely.

During Ike's illnesses, relations between the United States and the Soviet Union were far from smooth, and on the home front, civil-rights demonstrations were becoming more frequent. Openness about the president's medical problems did not exacerbate these situations, and perhaps it gave the president even more credibility with the public, officials, and foreign leaders. Of course, there was no guarantee that this would be the outcome, but Eisenhower was willing to take the risk. Also, he was a laid-back rather than hands-on president, so others were accustomed to taking his general directives and carrying them out. The illness of presidents who were more involved in the day-to-day running of the government would probably have different consequences.

PRESIDENTIAL RETREATS

One out of every five presidents has died in office, at the average age of fifty-seven, or died within five years after retirement, at the average age of sixty; while pre-Civil War presidents lived on average to seventy-three, the average declined by ten years for post-Civil War presidents.[12] Many First Ladies have recognized that the presidency is the world's most demanding job and have tried to keep their husbands from overworking. It is no wonder that these presidential wives have been concerned about their husband's well-being and devised a number of stratagems to keep them rested and healthy.

Several First Ladies urged their husbands to accompany them to presidential retreats to remove them from the favor-seekers, politicians, and reporters who flocked to the Oval Office at the White House and their summer vacation homes. Mary Lincoln took Abraham to rural Anderson Cottage at the Soldiers' Home in a rural area near Washington, D.C. Forty or so years later, Edith Roosevelt purchased "Pine Knot" cabin, 125 miles from Washington in the Blue Ridge Mountains of Virginia, where Theodore could indulge his love of nature. For the Franklin Roosevelts, there was Shangri La in Maryland, 75 miles (120km) from Washington. It had been built as a summer camp for children in the 1930s by the Civilian Conservation Corps, one of Franklin's government employment projects. It was refitted for the president in 1942, when World War II made it unsafe for him to take the presidential yacht out into the Atlantic Ocean. Originally named for a novel that described a secret paradise where people never aged, the presidential retreat was rechristened Camp David by the Eisenhowers to honor their only grandson.

Tender Loving Care

First Ladies also took steps to ensure that their husbands led healthier lives. At ten-thirty at night, Edith Roosevelt could be heard calling "The-o-dore," reminding the president to abandon the book he was usually reading and come to bed.[13] She also had tennis courts constructed at the White House to keep him trim. William Howard Taft's weight, some 350 pounds, troubled his wife, Nellie. A specially large bathtub had to be brought to the White House for his use. She put him on diets, but they did no good because he and his friends connived to eat all the forbidden foods when they went out or when he was aboard his private train. Taft had another health problem, narcolepsy, or the ability to fall asleep any time, anywhere. Seated near him, Nellie would prod him awake at dinners, conferences, and even cabinet meetings. She would also remind him of his official appointments since he tended to be absentminded.

Other presidential wives also protected their husbands. In 1928, when Grace Coolidge noticed how much medication her husband was taking for his asthma, she consulted the president's doctor because she thought it was unnecessary. She went on to limit his speaking engagements without his knowledge. Lady Bird Johnson worried about her husband's health because he had suffered a heart attack before he became president and tended to overwork. To get him to eat regularly, she would walk in on his meetings, bringing sandwiches. She noted in her diary that she hoped that "I can somehow be tactful enough, and gay enough, and sometimes even mean enough, to get Lyndon home at a reasonable hour for dinner and bed, or at least to get him to come home, bringing with him the documents of his office, so that he can work here in a more relaxed atmosphere."[14] Nancy Reagan insisted that she and her husband be served bottled water, juices, and decaffeinated coffee when they were not attending official dinners. Knowing Bill Clinton's preference for fast foods and his tendency to gain weight, Hillary ordered healthier foods served at the White House. As these many examples suggest, keeping their husbands healthy has been no easy task for First Ladies, especially if the president was a workaholic, a situation faced privately by many American wives.

▮▮▮▮▮▮▮ SEVEN ▮▮▮▮▮▮▮▮

HITTING THE
CAMPAIGN TRAIL

*"My husband gives the speeches,
and I receive the roses."*
—Lou Hoover

In the presidential race of 1824, none of the four candidates received a majority of the votes, forcing the House of Representatives to decide who the next president would be. John Quincy Adams, one of the contenders, gave his wife, Louisa, the task of campaigning for his election since she was more sociable than he. Louisa, the daughter of an American father and a British mother, had not even seen the United States until her husband brought her to the family home in Massachusetts in 1801, when she was twenty-six years old. At the age of forty-nine, she found herself immersed in American politics while her husband remained in the background. This was a reversal of the traditional roles of husband and wife in early nineteenth-century politics.

Every morning, John Quincy gave her a list of congressmen's wives to visit, often twenty-five in a day. Befriending them was one way to convince their husbands to vote for John Quincy, but it was a grueling task. She noted in her diary, "Oh these visits have made me sick many times, and I sometimes think they will make me crazy."[1] She also had to receive callers who came to meet her husband, another time-consuming task. She hosted dinners for sixty-eight members of Congress and held an open house every Tuesday night from May to December. In addition, she traveled to Philadelphia, where she met with noted journalists and congressmen and criticized outgoing President James Monroe's cabinet, in which her husband served as secretary of state. She also paid visits to Maryland and sought supporters for her husband. When she was in the capital, she often attended congressional debates. Known for her intellect and charm, Louisa was frequently asked for her opinion on current events.

In December 1823, John Quincy Adams decided that he and his wife should give a lavish ball to honor one of his presidential rivals, Andrew Jackson, on January 8, 1824, the anniversary of Jackson's 1814 victory over the British in the Battle of New Orleans. With less than three weeks to prepare, Louisa wrote, "I objected much to the plan but was overpowered by John's argument and the thing was settled."[2] While continuing with her regular round of social calls and dinners, she made arrangements for the ball and issued invitations to about 1,400 people; 1,000 eventually came. The gala evening at the Adams's home attracted much praise for its elegance and conviviality, but it probably did not make John Quincy Adams president. In all likelihood, what turned the tide in his favor was a deal he made with Henry Clay, another one of his opponents. Adams offered him the post of secretary of state in exchange for the votes Clay controlled, an arrangement soon labeled the "Corrupt Bargain."

Like Louisa Adams, Eleanor Roosevelt was ahead of her times as a political campaigner. For almost a decade, she had been involved with feminists and trade unionists, seeking to improve working conditions for women. She could mobilize their support for her husband's candidacy.

During Franklin's presidential races, Eleanor worked quietly behind the scenes, organizing the Women's Division of the Democratic Party and arranging for a woman in every state to take charge of feminine concerns and report directly to her. She also used her influence to win parity for the women on the platform committee, which prepared the party's stand on issues. In addition, Eleanor got the male politicians to accept the women's "Rainbow Fliers," educational campaign literature written by and for women, which stressed facts rather than party rhetoric. Eleanor was the first presidential candidate's wife to wield so much power within the party organization.

In 1940, Franklin even sent Eleanor to the unruly Democratic nominating convention to restore party unity when party delegates threatened to reject liberal cabinet member Henry A. Wallace, his choice for vice president. Confidently addressing the party delegates, she got them to accept her husband's choice of Wallace, "You cannot treat it as you would an ordinary nomination in an ordinary time. . . .This is a time when it is the United States we fight for."[3] Unspoken was the thought that her husband might not live to complete a third term. Later, during the campaign, the Republicans tried to make her an issue by handing out "We Don't Want Eleanor Either" buttons, the first time a president's wife was singled out for such treatment.

During Franklin's last campaign in 1944, she could say, much as she had during his first in 1932, " I have been very busy making 'non-political' speeches about registering and voting!"[4] Of course, she had accomplished a great deal more. In twelve years, she had made the Democratic Party more accessible to women, given a speech to the nominating convention, and delivered her husband's messages to voters. Ahead of her times, she had blazed a trail for future presidential wives.

THE STAY-AT-HOMES

Louisa Adams's achievement was remarkable when contrasted with the role most wives of presidential candidates played until late in

A candidate's wife became very important during the late 1800s. This cartoon shows Grover Cleveland being carried to the White House by his wife, Frances.

William and Ida McKinley ran a front-porch campaign in 1896.

the twentieth century. For most of the nineteenth century, women were not expected to participate in their husbands' campaigns although they often worked behind the scenes, making banners and cooking food for political meetings. In 1880, they became more visible when presidential candidates began to conduct "front-porch" campaigns, greeting visitors and giving speeches at homes. Their wives were often at their side, shaking hands and making polite conversation.

James and Crete Garfield initiated the front-porch campaign, and Crete became the first candidate's wife whose photograph appeared on a campaign poster. Around 300,000 people came to Caroline and Benjamin Harrison's home in Indianapolis when he ran for president in 1888. William McKinley also conducted a front-porch campaign in 1896. Despite Ida McKinley's infrequent appearances, she soon became known to the public. Her photograph appeared on campaign buttons, badges, and posters. She was the first candidate's wife to have a campaign biography written about her—to counter rumors that she was insane or a victim of wife-beatings because her public appearances were so rare. Her epileptic seizures were concealed from the public.

In Warren Harding's 1920 front-porch campaign, his wife, Florence, thrust herself into the spotlight. She was willing to offer a few impromptu remarks to the crowds that came to greet her husband, breaking the tradition that presidential candidates' wives might be seen but not heard. Florence had even attended the Republican nominating convention, where she persuaded uncommitted delegates to support her husband and surprised members of the press by seeking them out and answering their questions. As the former circulation manager of her husband's newspaper in Marion, Ohio, she was comfortable around reporters and often referred to them as "my boys."[5]

Although it was still unseemly for women to be active in their husbands' campaigns, Florence planned Warren's strategy. When a rumor circulated that some of her husband's ancestors were African-Americans, she rebuffed curious reporters by declaring, "I'm telling all you people that Warren Harding is not going to make any statement."[6] Since women were voting for the first time, Florence encouraged her husband to appeal directly to them, and she urged women to get involved in politics. She was the first presidential wife to vote for her husband for president.

On the Road

Candidates' wives became much more prominent when their husbands began to take train trips across the nation to appeal for votes. Although he lost the election of 1896, Democrat William Jennings Bryan became the first presidential candidate to deliver his message by railroad. He was accompanied by his wife. The wives of presidential candidates soon found themselves on display beside their husbands on campaign trains that crisscrossed the nation. Lou Hoover summed up the experience stating, "My husband gives the speeches, and I receive the roses."[7]

In 1948, First Lady Bess Truman participated in a cross-country campaign trip. On the train, she served as her husband's campaign advisor, mainly reviewing his speeches, but she also made sure that he ate and rested. A very private person, she preferred to stay out of the spotlight, but she soon grew accustomed to greeting crowds of small-town Americans gathered at each train stop. Harry introduced her to them as "the Boss," a title she disliked but accepted. By using this term, her husband was paying her a tribute his audiences understood. He was acknowledging that while she would usually keep her opinions to herself in public, in private she would certainly let him know what she was thinking.

Bess's successor, Mamie Eisenhower, was more comfortable traveling around the country with her husband. She happily granted interviews, met local politicians, and enjoyed being introduced to the public after her husband's speeches. Of course, he never called her "the Boss." Mamie became the first candidate's wife to have official campaign songs written about her. Taking the campaign on the road, whether by train or plane, became an American tradition, and in 1992, Hillary Clinton even traveled with her husband, Bill, on a political bus tour, a feat they repeated in 1996.

For years, when candidates' wives were interviewed by reporters, they would praise their husbands but avoid speaking out on controversial issues. Typical was Pat Nixon's comment to reporters, "I don't think one person can speak for another. The candidate should speak for himself."[8] Wives sat silently on the podium looking attractive and attentive while their husbands spoke, even if they had listened to the same speech in a number of different cities during the campaign. As late as the 1980s, reporters spoke about "the gaze," referring to the way Nancy Reagan cast adoring eyes on her husband, Ronald, when he delivered a speech. In 1992, Barbara Bush joked about the situation at a campaign luncheon she attended with her husband, George. After he introduced her, she got up to speak and told her audience, "See if he looks at me adoringly—as I looked at him."[9]

Television gave presidential candidates' wives greater visibility by bringing them into the homes of millions of Americans, about 90 million homes by 1960.[10] In the 1960 presidential race, both Jackie Kennedy and Pat Nixon were interviewed before the cameras, and their public appearances were also televised. Pat appeared stiff and wooden on the home screen and was labeled "Plastic Pat" by her detractors, although she was warm and personable when meeting people face-to-face. On camera, Jackie Kennedy's whispery, childlike voice contrasted with her elegant clothes and sophisticated style.

During the campaign, the Republican Party briefly turned the race into a duel between the candidates' wives by issuing a press release claiming, "When you elect a President, you are also electing a First Lady," and a columnist wrote that "for the first time in American history one woman could conceivably swing a presidential election."[11] Contrasting Pat's political experience as the wife of a vice president with Jackie's relative inexperience as a senator's wife, the Republicans sponsored "Pat Week" in October, holding rallies in her honor and distributing Pat-Nixon-for-First-Lady buttons while she continued to accompany her husband on the campaign trail. When criticized for being so politically active, she replied that being a campaigner was "reflective of women all over America taking an active part, not only in political life, but in all activities."[12] Since she was pregnant during the campaign, Jackie Kennedy limited her schedule of public appearances and made appeals to the voters by writing a news sheet called "Campaign Wife," distributed by the Democratic Party, and by taping speeches for broadcast on the radio, asking different ethnic groups in American society to register and vote. At that time, hers was the more traditional role, but that is not necessarily the reason why her husband won the election.

ON THEIR OWN

Candidates' wives had yet to campaign on their own until Lady Bird Johnson boarded the *Ladybird Special* to win votes for her husband, Lyndon, in October 1964. She called it "the four most dramatic days in my political life."[13] He had signed the Civil Rights Act, which antagonized the South by sweeping away discrimination in employment and public accommodations. As a Texan, she hoped to convince Southerners to remain in the Democratic Party. She traveled from Virginia to Louisiana, giving forty-seven speeches at sixty-seven stops, defending her husband's decision.[14] Prior to the trip, Lady Bird phoned Southern senators and asked them to join her on the train, and although many of them did not agree with her husband, they accepted her invitation. How much her trip contributed to Lyndon's victory, however, cannot be determined.

No longer would the wives of presidential candidates merely sit beside their husbands and smile. Rosalynn Carter even went out on her own to campaign for her husband in the primaries, elections that select the party's presidential candidates. She wrote, "It was like a job, a very demanding job, with pressures and deadlines."[15] Her successors followed her example. With so many states holding primaries, the wives often made speeches and raised funds in one section of the country while their husbands made appearances elsewhere. When presidents had to remain in Washington, their wives proved to be capable substitutes for them in primary campaigns.

Nevertheless, Hillary Rodham Clinton found herself without a role model when her husband described his 1992 presidential bid as "two for the price of one." No other political couple had openly admitted that they functioned as a team. She spoke so authoritatively on issues like children and health care that sometimes she seemed more qualified to be the presidential candidate than her husband. Furthermore, unlike other presidential wives, she was her family's main breadwinner, financial planner, and policy advocate.

Rosalynn Carter's heavy workload rarely left her any free time.

Reporters did not know how to treat her and often presented her as a hard, driven careerist. "I hardly recognized myself," she said.[16]

The Republican opposition attacked her own independent record of achievements (see Chapter One). For example, they condemned her for destroying family values by quoting her work for the Children's Defense Fund out of context to claim that she supported the right of children to sue their parents over minor matters. She decided to ignore these attacks because the explanations would prove too complex and detailed to be covered accurately in the media or to be easily grasped by the public. However, she confronted stories about her husband's infidelity directly, appearing on television to convince the public that the Clintons had a solid, loving marriage (see Chapter Five). She also softened her image and followed advice from the Clinton campaign strategists to play up her roles as a caring mother and a loving wife, rather than as a capable policymaker, legal wizard, and advocate of reforms. In the 1996 campaign, she kept a low profile, attracting less controversy and media attention.

The wives of presidential candidates have come a long way. No longer are they hidden at home, nor are they expected to display themselves mutely beside their husbands. Nevertheless, Hillary Clinton's experience suggests that the American public has not yet come to terms with the next step—First Ladies who have careers and their own record of achievements. With 61.6 percent of American women projected to be working in the year 2000,[17] future First Ladies will have to deal with this problem, learning from the difficulties Hillary faced and the way she handled them.

EIGHT

TAKING UP CAUSES

One must not do too much for people, but one must help them to do for themselves.
—*Eleanor Roosevelt*

Entering the White House during the Progressive Era, a period noted for its reforms of business, politics, and quality of life, Ellen Wilson insisted that First Ladies should have a public social-work project and chose slum clearance as hers. During the seventeen months that she was First Lady, she tried to improve living conditions for poor African-Americans in the nation's capital, where homes were often unsanitary hovels hidden in alleys behind Washington streets. In 1913, Charlotte Hopkins of the National Civic Federation asked for her help in ridding the capital of these slums and arranged for her to tour the rat-infested, disease-ridden firetraps. In response to what she saw, Ellen bought shares in a housing company that built model homes for the poor and became the honorary chairwoman of the National Civic Federation. She also hosted a reception for members of Congress and housing reformers to enable them to discuss the issue face-to-face. A longtime southerner, she did not favor equality for African-Americans, but as a minister's daughter, she felt it was her Christian duty to help the less fortunate.

Under her leadership, a bill was drafted and sent to Congress for action; however, it stalled once it was discovered that many of the alleys were owned by their inhabitants, not by profiteering real estate companies. The bill was flawed because it proposed to clear the slums and convert them into parks and streets but made no provision for housing the blacks who would lose their homes. By August 1914, Ellen was bedridden, dying from a kidney disease, but the slum clearance bill was still on her mind, and she told her husband, "I would go away more peacefully if my Alley Bill was passed by Congress."[1] Just before her death on August 7, she was told that Congress had honored her wish.

When she became First Lady during the Great Depression, Eleanor Roosevelt revived interest in Ellen Wilson's project by helping to bring more slum-clearance laws before Congress and by taking congressional wives on tours of the alleys. The resulting Alley Dwelling Act received enough funding to clear only a quarter of the hovels because at that time low-cost housing for the poor was deemed less important than other public works projects. Eleanor did not lose interest in public housing, however, and in 1933, she sponsored Arthurdale, a model community for unemployed West Virginia miners in poverty-stricken Morgantown

Eleanor Roosevelt (left) arranged for Marian Anderson to perform "The Star Spangled Banner" *in front of the Lincoln Memorial.*

designed to promote self-sufficiency by providing a factory, post office, inexpensive housing, and schools. She became personally involved in Arthurdale's development, hiring personnel, soliciting contributions, and making frequent inspection tours. When critics in Congress reduced funding, the community was doomed, but its goal of providing children with decent homes and improved opportunities survived. In 1936, Eleanor summed up what she had learned from the venture. "There is always grave danger in anything that is experimental. One must not do too much for people, but one must help them to do for themselves."[2]

During her twelve years as First Lady, Eleanor Roosevelt was involved in a number of different projects, but these were often an extension of her interest in people, an interest she had developed as a young socialite in 1903 and then shared with Franklin. Throughout his political career, she brought the plight of the downtrodden to his attention and appealed to his conscience to do something about their problems. Although she often wanted to go farther and faster than her husband would or could, her recommendations were consistent with his programs and views of government. Through her numerous press conferences with women reporters, her radio talks, and newspaper columns, she was able to focus public attention on the causes she adopted, but she still faced stiff opposition and widespread criticism.

Among Eleanor's myriad interests were her involvement with youth, her crusade for civil rights, and her concern for European refugees during World War II. The Depression left American youth with little hope of employment or higher education. When Franklin Roosevelt set up the Civilian Conservation Corps in 1933, putting young people to work on reforestation, irrigation, and flood control, Eleanor insisted that young women be included to do lighter tasks, and she encouraged the first female cabinet member, Secretary of Labor Frances Perkins, to set up a camp for them at Bear Mountain, New York. In 1935, she helped to develop the National Youth Administration (NYA), a government agency to give jobs to unemployed young people and part-time work to high school and college students. The First Lady came under fire for her support and close association with the American Youth Congress, an increasingly left-wing reform group. On the one hand, she conspicuously appeared in support of one former member when he testified before a hostile congressional committee, but on the other hand, she bawled these young people out when they openly mouthed Soviet propaganda. By 1939, she began to spend less time with them.

In 1939, Eleanor resigned from the Daughters of the American Revolution (DAR) because they refused to let African-American opera soprano Marian Anderson sing in their Constitution Hall. At the time Washington, D.C., was racially segregated, a fact Eleanor deplored. In a well-publicized gesture of support, the First Lady arranged for Ms. Anderson to perform on the steps of the Lincoln Memorial before an audience of around 75,000. She also asked the soprano to sing before the king and queen of England during their visit to the Roosevelt home in Hyde Park, New York.

Eleanor also fought to get blacks jobs in the government and in defense industries as war clouds gathered in the late 1930s and early 1940s. She frequently worked behind the scenes to improve their lot while she counseled blacks to be patient. Despite opposition from Southern members of Congress, she fervently backed the Anti-Lynching Bill to end the murder of blacks by white terrorists. Her mentor and friend was Mary McLeod Bethune, chief of the National Youth Administration's Division of Negro Affairs, with whom she attended a segregated meeting in Birmingham, Alabama. Seated beside Ms. Bethune, Eleanor was told to move over to the section reserved for whites, but she simply moved her chair over to an aisle.

Earlier she had spoken out on behalf of improving economic and educational opportunities for African-Americans, but gradually she also realized that integration had to replace segregation. In 1941, she wrote, "I have long felt that many of the things we deplore, . . . are not due just to lack of education and to physical differences, but are due in great part to the basic fact of segregation which we have set up in this country and which warps and twists the lives not only of our Negro population, but sometimes of foreign born or even of religious groups."[3] She included black educators and activists as well as sharecroppers as her dinner guests at the Executive Mansion.

In 1940, after the fall of France to German forces, Eleanor heeded the pleas of scientist Albert Einstein and other famous European refugees to help those who wanted to emigrate to the United States. State Department bureaucrats, fearful of antagonizing Congress and the public, made it difficult for refugees to get entry permits. Eleanor took up their cause with sympathetic Assistant Secretary of State Sumner Welles and with her husband. She tried to assist intellectuals, trade union leaders, and members of the underground who were desperate to leave Europe. The most endangered got emergency visas, but despite her prodding, progress was slow. When she heard rumors about the Holocaust, there was little she could do, but she did protest the internment of Japanese-Americans in concentration camps and even visited one camp in Arizona. It was often said that in supporting so many causes, Eleanor served as the conscience of the Roosevelt administration.

TRADITIONAL PROJECTS

Ellen Wilson's project fell within the traditional role ascribed to women while Eleanor Roosevelt's social and political activism blazed a new trail that many of her successors were reluctant to follow. First Ladies who advocated political and legal change met with resistance. In the eighteenth century, Abigail Adams was ahead of her time when she pleaded with her husband, John, to improve women's rights. As a traditionalist, he held the view that women were dependents, not capable, self-reliant adults, and he failed to act upon her request.

Twentieth-century First Ladies gradually became more outspoken in their support for feminism as women's movements gained strength and began to achieve their objectives. Nellie Taft supported higher education for women as well as the right to vote, but she did not think women should hold office because it would disrupt their family life. After women gained the vote in 1920, Florence Harding accepted an honorary membership in the National Women's Party, which in 1923 sponsored the first Equal Rights Amendment (ERA) to eliminate discrimination between the sexes, and she invited members of women's political groups to the White House. Lou Hoover encouraged women to enter politics as well as to vote. She also encouraged them to engage in competitive athletics. Eleanor Roosevelt was a living example of an empowered woman, but she opposed the ERA because she felt women workers needed laws to protect them from oppressive working conditions. Some of her successors, like Rosalynn Carter and Betty Ford, continued to press for women's rights by supporting a new version of the ERA in the 1970s and 1980s.

It is claimed that First Ladies became involved in social causes during the nineteenth century as an outgrowth of the belief that women were more moral and sensitive than men.[4] Their charitable deeds on behalf of the less fortunate were socially acceptable activities, extending the values of home life to the larger community. Thus Dolley Madison's efforts to found the Washington City Orphans Asylum in 1815 were considered praiseworthy. Concern with wounded soldiers and needy veterans was another appropriate area of feminine activity. First Lady Mary Lincoln devoted herself to this cause. Mary stepped out of bounds, however, because she illegally diverted funds from the soldiers to African-Americans. In 1863, she became involved in the Contraband Relief Association, a private group that provided welfare for needy former slaves. Although a Southerner by birth, Mary had become an abolitionist in 1862 and urged her husband to free the slaves months before he finally signed the Emancipation Proclamation in 1863. In the early 1920s, even avowed feminist Florence Harding visited soldiers wounded during World War I and entertained them at the White House. However, she relied too much upon Charles Forbes, Director of the Veterans Bureau, who was later discovered to have been selling hospital supplies purchased by the government for his own profit.

Twentieth-century First Ladies, for the most part, followed in the footsteps of their nineteenth-century counterparts and continued to promote causes associated with family, community, and patriotic values. Eleanor Roosevelt was one of very few to embrace political activism, and even she was often advocating policies that would support and extend her husband's programs. Most of her successors chose to support less controversial causes and made sure that these dovetailed with their husband's policies or philosophies of government.

Eleanor's immediate predecessors, First Ladies Grace Coolidge and Lou Hoover, were attracted to children's issues. Grace had taught deaf children at the Clarke Institute for the Deaf before she married Calvin Coolidge in 1903. She often invited students from the school to the White House and tried to publicize their problems. Her efforts helped make Americans more sensitive to the needs of the disabled, a position her husband shared. She was also active on behalf of the Campfire Girls and the Association for the Aid of Crippled Children and encouraged the production of movies suitable for children to see.

Lou Hoover became a supporter of children's causes.

Lou Hoover became the honorary chairperson of the Girl Scouts, inviting them to the White House and personally financing some of their programs. After the stock market crashed in 1929 and the nation plunged into the Great Depression, Lou tried to help women and children secure adequate food and clothing. To reach them, she became the first presidential wife to speak over the radio. For example, in 1931 she told children to "take concern for the welfare of others' lives. This year, more than usual, there are more people in need of special care."[5] She encouraged their self-reliance and volunteerism, principles her husband Herbert preferred to government intervention and assistance.

PET PROJECTS

After Eleanor Roosevelt left the White House, presidential wives became less visible and more focused on private concerns rather than social projects. They reflected a national trend that encouraged women to find fulfillment at home once their husbands, fathers, sons, and brothers returned home from the battlefields of World War II. In 1960, Jackie Kennedy, unlike her immediate predecessors, developed a project of her own, but it echoed the domestic themes of the past rather than the activism that characterized the era. She decided to restore original furnishings to the White House, explaining, "Presidents' wives have an obligation to contribute something. People who visit the White House see practically nothing that dates before 1900. People should see things that develop their sense of history."[6] Her project complemented her husband's goal of making Washington, D.C., the cultural as well as the governmental capital of the nation.

Jackie Kennedy was personally involved in her restoration project. She scoured a government warehouse for antiques; formed a White House Fine Arts Advisory Committee; convinced Congress to pass a law protecting the antiques, declaring the White House a museum, and allowing the Executive Mansion to accept donations; decided what should be accepted or rejected; appointed a curator for the collection; and appealed to wealthy Americans to return possessions of former White House occupants. Jackie was instrumental in establishing the White House Historical Association, which publishes information about the Mansion and acquires additional objects for it. She wrote a guidebook for the Association to educate the public and raise funds for ongoing acquisitions.

In February 1962, Jackie shared her achievements with more than 48 million Americans by taking them on a television tour of the White House, explaining what had been restored in each room and describing the Mansion's history.[7] Her work was continued by Lady Bird Johnson and by Pat Nixon. Lady Bird encouraged her husband to provide permanent federal funds for the White House curator and set up the Committee for the Preservation of the White House. Pat worked quietly with the White House curator to double the number of antique furnishings in the Mansion. Rosalynn Carter helped establish the White House Trust Fund, to provide permanent funds to purchase antiques for the Mansion and continue Jackie Kennedy's work.

In 1964, after her husband was elected president, Lady Bird decided to develop her own project, the beautification of the nation, a theme Lyndon Johnson had mentioned in a message to Congress.

Her object was to clean up and preserve the natural scenic landscape of the country. In 1965, she got Congress to pass the Highway Beautification Act to limit billboards on federal highways. To promote her project, Lady Bird also sponsored a White House Conference on Natural Beauty, gave speeches linking crime with squalor, appeared on a television special, and encouraged those interested in the environment, philanthropy, and design to help her.

"This is the Year of the Shovel for me!" she proclaimed.[8] She traveled over 100,000 miles (160,000km) on forty different trips to plant trees and flowers and dedicate new parks and gardens.[9] Like Ellen Wilson and Eleanor Roosevelt, she, too, was concerned with Washington's alley shanties and encouraged beautification projects in the slums, encouraging poor people to help themselves. She also worked to improve landscaping in the nation's capital, armed with private donations of plants and money as well as help from the Park Service. She planted cherry trees, much as First Lady Nellie Taft had done. Nellie had arranged to have Potomac Drive turned into a promenade, like one she admired during her stay in the Philippines, and she inaugurated the annual cherry blossom festival, which became a tourist attraction.

Lady Bird's successor, Pat Nixon, did not focus on a particular project. She encouraged volunteerism by traveling around the nation to give recognition and encouragement to people who freely donated their time and money to improve society. She also received them at the White House. Despite her interest in nonpolitical causes, Pat was the first presidential wife to publicly support passage of a new ERA, proposed in 1972.

Her replacement, Betty Ford, took up a traditional project as First Lady—the Washington Hospital for Sick Children—but it was her outspoken views on controversial issues affecting women that attracted national attention. An ardent feminist, she worked for the ERA and even phoned state legislators to get them to approve the amendment. "When Jerry became President, I kept pushing, trying to influence him," she wrote,[10] and he did sign an order with moral, if not legal, force against legal inequalities between the sexes. Her husband did not share all her feminist views, but that did not stop her from expressing opinions on premarital sex, the right of women to terminate unwanted pregnancies, and the drug problem, during a television interview in August 1975. It was her

Betty Ford devoted herself to passing the Equal Rights Amendment.

willingness to discuss her breast cancer surgery in 1974, however, that endeared her to the American public and undoubtedly saved thousands of lives by encouraging women to have checkups.

Aside from her interest in mental health (see Chapter Nine), Rosalynn Carter was especially concerned about the problems of the elderly. She visited nursing homes and senior centers and invited advocates of the elderly to White House conferences on aging. Her testimony before Congress helped produce the Older Americans Act, increasing funds for social services and health programs for the elderly, and the Age Discrimination Act, eliminating mandatory retirement in government and raising the retirement age from 65 to 70 in the private sector. Rosalynn also fought for passage of the ERA, but in 1982, however, time ran out. Three states short of approval, the amendment failed. Rosalynn considered this her "greatest disappointment in all the projects I worked on during the White House years."[11] Among the other projects she sponsored were programs for children and minorities.

When Barbara Bush became First Lady, she continued to be a spokesperson for literacy, a project she had begun in 1981. This rather traditional, noncontroversial project was well suited to her grandmotherly image. She became interested in literacy after working with a learning-disabled son who had difficulty reading. Then, she discovered that illiteracy could create a number of social problems, such as homelessness and crime. As First Lady, Barbara prepared a book about her dog Millie's views of what it was like to live with the presidential couple and donated the proceeds to the Barbara Bush Foundation for Family Literacy. In addition, she hosted conferences and made speeches on behalf of literacy. Barbara also demonstrated her concern for the innocent victims of AIDS. Reporters and photographers showed her picking up and kissing an AIDS baby, viewing a national patchwork quilt in memory of AIDS victims, and placing candles in the White House windows during an AIDS commemoration night at the Lincoln Memorial. These were causes future First Ladies might adopt. Unlike some of her predecessors, she chose not to speak out on controversial issues, such as gun control and a woman's right to terminate an unwanted pregnancy, to avoid public disagreements with her husband.

First Ladies have been criticized for doing too much or doing too little. Although their service to the public is strictly voluntary and their title is merely honorary, they have used the power of their own positions, the publicity their actions received, and their access to the president to contribute to American life. Presidential wives have championed underprivileged, sick, elderly, female, minority, and young Americans. They have worked to improve living conditions for all and to preserve the nation's ties to its past. Whether it is desirable or possible for future First Ladies to continue these activities remains to be seen, especially if they decide to pursue their own careers during their husbands' presidency.

▮▮▮▮▮▮▮▮ NINE ▮▮▮▮▮▮▮▮▮

PRESENTING TWO FOR THE PRICE OF ONE

My husband and I have always been each other's sounding boards

—Hillary Clinton

When James K. Polk became president, his wife Sarah said, "He set me to work too."[1] Childless and uninterested in homemaking, she was the perfect political partner for James as he moved up the political ladder from the Tennessee legislature to Congress. She was well educated, having attended Moravian Female Academy, an outstanding women's school in Salem, North Carolina, and well informed, having listened with growing interest to discussions of current events conducted by her father, a local politician, at the family plantation in Tennessee. Sarah critiqued her husband's speeches and discussed policies with him in an upstairs office they shared in the White House. He regarded newspapers as important indicators of public opinion and asked her to read them and select articles for his attention.

While Sarah Polk served as her husband's assistant, she never sought recognition for her work and concealed her role in shaping American history. In 1845, when the Polks entered the White House, women were not expected to participate in politics or draw unseemly attention to themselves. The Polks had seen firsthand the damage malicious gossip could do when a woman came under public scrutiny, for they were aware that it hastened the death of President Andrew Jackson's wife, Rachel, who may have been briefly guilty of unintentional bigamy. Always proper and discreet, Sarah credited her husband with the views she expressed in public and the policies the government pursued. She preferred discussions of politics to social gossip, however, so she frequently deserted her female guests at the White House to join with their husbands in commenting on the issues of the day.

Although her own political preferences were not recorded, it is known that this deeply religious woman shared her husband's belief in the "Manifest Destiny" of the United States, the belief that the United States was ordained to expand across the North American continent. Under the Polks, the nation gained an additional 800,000 square miles (2,000,000 square km) of land, most of it the result of the Mexican War (1846–1848). Sarah considered this "one of the most important events in the history of this country."[2] James discussed the conduct of the war and the treaty negotiations with her because she was the only one he trusted. His secretary of state, James Buchanan, had opposed the conflict. The Polks worked so hard that Sarah fell seriously ill several times during their White House years and her husband died soon after leaving office.

One hundred years later, Bess Truman served as her husband Harry's silent presidential partner. She was even more self-effacing than Sarah Polk, and the public hardly knew that Bess was helping Harry do his job. She preferred anonymity because she had experienced firsthand the pain caused by publicity and gossip. Tabloid newspaper stories following her father's suicide when she was eighteen left her fearful and suspicious of reporters. Later, editorials criticizing Eleanor Roosevelt and her children gave Bess another reason to preserve her privacy.

Bess had been helping Harry since he started in politics by clipping local newspaper articles for him when he was out of town, talking over political matters with him, and sometimes by managing his office. When he became a senator, she was put on his office payroll. After Franklin Roosevelt's sudden death thrust Harry into the presidency in April 1945, Bess was temporarily cast aside. Her husband was too busy to consult her while he was being briefed on Roosevelt's policies for ending World War II and learning to master his new responsibilities. When he returned to the family home in Independence, Missouri, for Christmas, Bess finally vented her frustration at being excluded from her advisory role by snapping at him, "As far as I'm concerned, you might as well have stayed in Washington."[3]

When she returned to the White House, they began the new year as political partners. From then on, every night that they did not have to attend an official function, she would join him after dinner in his study for discussions of the issues, personalities, and problems he faced. Harry Truman insisted that his wife was "a full partner in all my transactions—politically and otherwise." She was his sounding board for the creation of the Marshall Plan in 1947 to rebuild war-torn Europe, the military intervention in South Korea to repel an invasion from the North Koreans in 1950, and other momentous decisions. He claimed, "I discussed them all with her. . . . Her judgment was always good, and she never made a suggestion that wasn't for the welfare and benefit of the country and what I was trying to do."[4] When they differed over an issue, such as his intention to run for election in 1948, she did not nag him to have her way but quietly supported his decision.

Bess was also the censor of his public statements. Since he peppered his speeches with "hell" and "damn" and a variety of other swearwords, she was forever reprimanding him, "You shouldn't have said that!"[5] The public, however, grew to like Harry's salty language. During his 1948 presidential campaign, they would even shout, "Give 'em hell, Harry!" sentiments Bess might applaud even if she did not approve of the language.

Unlike most First Ladies, Edith Wilson and Nancy Reagan exercised great political power on their husband's behalf, but their efforts were primarily intended to protect their ailing mates (see Chapter Six). Eleanor Roosevelt, Rosalynn Carter, and Hillary Clinton were recognized as full political partners because they often acted as surrogates for their husbands in public. Eleanor had gone on inspection trips for her husband when he was governor of New York. A month after he became president, Franklin sent her to Appalachia to report on the terrible poverty afflicting the region. "Watch the people's faces. Look at the conditions of the clothes on the wash lines. You can tell a lot from that," the president instructed her.[6] During her husband's first two terms in office, she covered about 40,000 miles (64,000 km) yearly, even descending into mine shafts to see working conditions for herself and riding in buckets to survey progress on the construction of Boulder and Norris Dams. The president's speechwriters often turned to her for advice on consumer affairs or relief for the poor.

Not only did she supply her husband and his speechwriters with firsthand information, she made recommendations and bullied members of his cabinet and personal staff to make sure her husband's reforms were carried out. She also brought guests to the dinner table, seating them near Franklin, so that they could plead their causes directly to him. Sometimes her timing was bad, because Franklin looked forward to the dinner hour as a time for relaxation rather than politics.

Rosalynn Carter became the very active and visible honorary chairperson of the President's Commission on Mental Health. (She could not become the actual chairperson because in 1967 Congress passed a law preventing presidential family members from holding paid government positions.) She had developed a personal interest in mental health when her husband, Jimmy, was governor of Georgia. In addition to giving speeches on mental health, she had traveled the country collecting information and was the first presidential wife since Eleanor Roosevelt to testify before a Senate Committee. (Eleanor had been questioned about conditions facing miners in the 1940s.) She was pleased when Congress passed the Mental Health Systems Act in 1980.

Rosalynn served as an advisor to her husband, offering her opinions, bringing issues to his attention, and reviewing and rewriting his speeches. He acknowledged, "There's seldom a decision that I make that I don't first discuss with her. She's got superb political judgment."[7] They had a working lunch in the president's Oval Office every Wednesday. Despite objections from the press and political opponents, Rosalynn also sat in on cabinet meetings and met with cabinet officials individually to discuss items on her agenda, such as mental health. The meetings helped her to understand the details of policy and to stay on top of complex issues so that she could offer Jimmy more sound advice.

Hillary Rodham Clinton was an even more visible First Lady. The Clintons' campaign slogan had promised "Two for the Price of

One," and after the election of 1992, Bill Clinton put his wife to work, helping him select the individuals who would work with him in government. She became the first presidential wife to have an office in the West Wing of the White House, where the president worked, so that she and her husband could consult on matters of policy. "My husband and I have always been each other's sounding boards," Hillary admitted.[8] Eleanor Roosevelt was her role model, and Hillary even admitted to holding imaginary conversations with her idol as part of brainstorming sessions when she was writing a book. Hillary stated, " One thing I've learned since becoming First Lady is that wherever I go, Eleanor Roosevelt has surely been there before me."[9]

Soon after Bill was officially sworn in, he appointed her as the unpaid head of the president's Task Force on Health Care Reform,

"Two For the Price of One"—Hillary leads the initiative for health care reform.

based on her experience helping him when he was governor of Arkansas. In charge of six cabinet members as well as important White House aides, she was quickly embroiled in controversy. Task force hearings were not open to the public, so doctors who wanted to testify brought a lawsuit demanding to be heard and questioned the First Lady's right to head the group since she was not a government official. An appeals court ruled in Hillary's favor. This important decision gave legal recognition to First Ladies' quasi-government roles, referring to a "long-standing tradition of public service by First Ladies . . . who have acted (albeit in the background) as advisors and personal representatives of their husbands."[10] Hillary appeared before five different committees of Congress in one week, advocating health care measures to protect every American. She was armed with facts and figures but also spoke with warmth and compassion. However, neither Congress nor the public was ready for a major overhaul in the health care system, and the proposal was defeated.

Hillary's political prominence stirred up controversies concerning events that took place before she became First Lady. At issue were Whitewater, the Clintons' Arkansas real-estate investment that soured, and Hillary's investment in cattle futures that yielded a large profit. She was not the first presidential wife to be questioned about her financial dealings, however. The House Banking Committee investigated Julia Grant for supposedly making a $25,000 profit when financiers attempted to corner the gold market in 1869, but nothing came of the charges.

Questions also arose concerning Hillary's possible role in concealing information about the suicide of her former law partner and White House aide, Vince Foster; the shredding of papers at her former law firm in Arkansas; and the firing of members of the White House Travel Office. She became the first presidential wife to testify before a federal grand jury, which was investigating whether the Clintons blocked efforts to obtain billing records from her former law firm, records that turned up unexpectedly at the White House living quarters. Investigators had been trying for months to locate them, and Hillary denied having any knowledge of where they were. While the novelty of having a successful career woman as First Lady might have provoked some of these attacks, they could also be seen as a way of criticizing her husband. Her actual involvement in these matters remained to be seen.

First Ladies were not always successful in getting their husbands to take the action they desired. Despite French attacks on American shipping and hostility toward American diplomats sent to negotiate the problem, John Adams withstood his wife Abigail's insistence that the United States declare war on France. James Polk remained steadfast in his opposition to chartering a national bank even though Sarah complained bitterly to friends, "Why, if we must use gold and silver all the time, a lady can scarcely carry enough money with her."[11] This was the only issue on which they disagreed in public. Millard Fillmore did not heed his wife Abigail's advice when he signed the Fugitive Slave Act of 1850, requiring the return of escaped slaves and penalizing those who helped them or failed to turn them in. Abigail had opposed the law on humanitarian grounds, but she also knew it would end her husband's political career.

MAKING HER VOICE HEARD

First Ladies also helped their husbands make political appointments. Often they were shrewder judges of character or more politically astute than the men they married. For example, Crete Garfield successfully persuaded her husband to appoint James Blaine as secretary of state, turning a rival for the presidential nomination into a valuable political ally. In 1933, Eleanor Roosevelt was responsible for getting the first woman named to a president's cabinet, Secretary of Labor Frances Perkins, and for placing women in lower-level government posts. To improve her husband's presidential image, in 1945 Bess Truman suggested that Harry appoint their old high school classmate, newspaperman Charlie Ross, as press secretary. Less lofty motives led First Ladies such as Abigail Adams, Julia Tyler, Mary Lincoln, and Julia Grant to get government jobs for members of their families. This was much easier to do before competitive examinations and more rigorous qualifications were instituted in the late 1880s.

Not only were First Ladies successful in influencing presidential appointments, they were often instrumental in firing members of their husbands' official family. For instance, in 1870 Julia Grant insisted that her husband dismiss Postmaster General Marshall Jewell, whom she saw as a potential rival if Ulysses chose to run for a third term. She maneuvered the resignation of Secretary of the Interior Jacob Cox because he supported competitive examinations for government service, a policy her husband opposed. Wanting to be her husband's sole confidante, in 1919 Edith Wilson successfully drove a wedge between Woodrow and his trusted advisor Colonel Edward M. House after Wilson became ill. She is also reputed to have convinced her husband to obtain the resignation of Secretary of State Lansing (see Chapter Six). Rosalynn Carter got her husband to dismiss Secretary of Health, Education, and Welfare Joseph Califano in 1979. In the 1980s, Nancy Reagan engineered the firing, resignation, and dismissal of those members of the administration who tarnished her husband's image as president or who failed to protect it sufficiently. Most of those who were forced to leave were conservative politicians and included one secretary of state, two secretaries of the interior, the secretary of health and human services, and a presidential chief of staff (See also Chapter 6 and 10).[12]

Sometimes presidents failed to take their wives' advice on appointees. For instance, in the 1860s Mary Lincoln could never convince her husband to dismiss Secretary of State William Seward or Treasury Secretary Salmon Chase, whose presidential ambitions she suspected. In 1904, Edith Roosevelt discouraged her husband from making William Howard Taft secretary of war because she believed he would not advise the president as impartially as his predecessor did. Theodore ignored her advice, but she proved to be correct. To Pat Nixon's great disappointment, in the 1970s her husband Richard did not appoint any women to the Supreme Court even though he had agreed to look into the matter.

In order to assist their husbands, twentieth-century First Ladies gradually entered the world of international diplomacy. From the earliest days of the republic they had graciously entertained visiting foreign dignitaries. Then they began to travel and were treated with the honors due the wife of a head of state. Finally they set forth on their own to represent the nation at ceremonial functions and to serve as the president's personal emissary on diplomatic missions.

Diplomatic Duties

Aside from hostessing state dinners for world leaders, Edith Roosevelt became a diplomat by proxy. She helped her husband bypass official channels by receiving informative letters about conditions in Russia on the eve of the Russo-Japanese War from a British diplomat posted in St. Petersburg. She shared their contents with Theodore who later received a Nobel Peace Prize for negotiating a settlement of the war in August 1905. In 1906, Edith and Theodore became the first presidential couple to travel outside the continental United States when they visited Panama to observe the construction of the canal.

Presidential wives began to travel abroad in 1919, when Edith Wilson became the first First Lady to visit Europe on an official trip with her husband. She attended the Paris Peace Conference ending World War I. Unlike the other leaders' wives, she was determined to assist her husband so she attended the daily American press briefings and reported back to him. She had to hide behind a curtain to witness the signing of the peace treaty because only official members of the Peace Commission were allowed to be present. Perhaps the most memorable First Lady to be honored as the wife of a visiting head of state was Jackie Kennedy, who accompanied her husband on an official visit to France in 1961. Her elegant clothes, as well as her ability to speak French, made such a hit in that fashion-conscious country that the president introduced himself as the "man who brought Jacqueline Kennedy to Paris."[13]

In 1972, Pat Nixon became the first presidential wife to visit West Africa, receiving a nineteen-gun salute as the official representative of the United States at the inauguration of William R. Tolbert as president of Liberia. She even donned the traditional dress of African women while watching ceremonial dances the next day. Before returning to the United States, she met with the heads of state of Ghana and the Ivory Coast, where she received enthusiastic welcomes. In 1974, she made another solo trip, this time to Venezuela and Brazil for the inaugurations of their presidents.

Rosalynn Carter was given even more diplomatic recognition and responsibility when she was sent to seven Latin American countries as the president's official envoy in 1977. After briefings by the State and Treasury Departments, the National Security Council, and the Organization of American States, she was well

Pat Nixon receives a makeover during her visit to Africa.

prepared. In addition, she had been taking Spanish classes. In each nation, she presented her husband's arguments in favor of establishing a nuclear-free zone in Latin America, discussed his strong commitment to human rights, and issued statements regarding American policy toward the host government. "At the end of each session with a leader, I would write a long memorandum to be wired back to the President and the State Department. I included virtually everything that had happened and been said, leaving it to the experts in Washington to interpret the information."[14]

She functioned as a professional diplomat, mediating a dispute between Peru and Ecuador and discussing the illegal drug trade in Colombia. She was accepted as the president's stand-in in the countries she visited. Although she was criticized as unqualified to serve as a diplomat, many American ambassadors had less diplomatic training than she and were appointed to their posts as a reward for their generous political contributions. Upon her return, the United States Senate congratulated her on the success of her mission.

In 1978, she also represented the president at the inaugurations of the presidents of Bolivia and Ecuador and the funeral of Pope

Paul VI. When the prime minister of Israel, Menachem Begin, and the president of Egypt, Anwar Sadat, came to Camp David to negotiate the Middle East Peace Accords, which granted recognition to Israel in exchange for land, Rosalynn met with their wives. She was kept informed of developments and made arrangements to hold the historic signing of the agreement on the White House lawn.

Her successors, Nancy Reagan and Barbara Bush, continued the practice of traveling on their own to ceremonial functions as their husbands' representatives, but they were not assigned any diplomatic missions. For example, Nancy attended the wedding of Prince Charles and Lady Diana Spencer in England, while Barbara went to the funeral of Japanese emperor Hirohito and led a delegation to the inauguration of Costa Rican president Rafael Calderon. Both First Ladies met with Raisa Gorbachev. While Nancy and Raisa tried to upstage one another in a competition that made headlines, Barbara enjoyed a more comfortable relationship with the wife of the Soviet leader. Neither relationship had any major diplomatic consequences.

First Ladies have always influenced their husbands, but it is their more recent public role as their husbands' political partners and as diplomats that has raised important questions. Are they qualified to perform government service at home or abroad? When they head up government task forces, should they be regarded as independent women or as spokespersons for their husbands? Should they be paid when they serve in an official capacity, such as directing a government commission? None of the women who openly assisted their husbands was an amateur. They had all been active earlier in their husbands' political or business careers, and two of the women had worked on their own while their husbands held state offices. As the number of American working wives increases, it is likely that future First Ladies will choose to exercise political power as their husband's partners, unless, of course, they prefer to devote themselves to their own careers while living in the White House. The days of a First Lady as a traditional silent partner have probably passed.

TEN

RUNNING AN OFFICE

Let's make these letters glow. I see them framed in hotels—from First Ladies and Presidents, and I want mine not to have any grammatical errors. I want them to be ones I'm proud of.

—Lady Bird Johnson

To conceal her anxiety, Eleanor Roosevelt passed around a big box of candied fruits to the thirty-five women reporters assembled in the Red Room for her first official press conference. She wanted to encourage the hiring of newspaper women, so men were excluded. The reporters had accepted her ground rules and agreed that their questions would focus on matters of interest to women. Actually, Eleanor's first formal meeting with the reporters was not especially newsworthy except that it marked the beginning of regularly scheduled conferences between First Ladies and journalists and started a new White House tradition. She gave 347 more such conferences before she left the White House.[1] In them, Eleanor took up substantive issues such as sweatshops, teachers' salaries, international cooperation, and healthy but money-saving menus. One reporter commented, "At the President's press conference, all the world's a stage; at Mrs. Roosevelt's, all the world's a school."[2]

Eleanor worked in her bedroom, but after construction of the East Wing was completed, she and her staff moved there, along with military and social aides. In time, the East Wing became a synonym for the Office of First Lady. Eleanor served as her own press secretary, publicizing matters she felt were important and creating her own public image. Unlike today's First Ladies, she had very little staff assistance and drew instead on the people serving her husband when she needed them. Most of the time she relied on a Edith Helm and Malvina "Tommy" Thompson. Tommy took dictation for Eleanor's news and magazine columns, and speeches. She also took care of Eleanor's mail, helped by 12 employees from the White House correspondence division. Eleanor received 300,000 letters from the public in 1933 and often got as many as 600 to 700 pieces of mail a day while she was First Lady.[3]

"I feel strongly that publicity in this era has gotten completely out of hand—you must really protect the privacy of me and my children—but not offend [the press],"[4] First Lady Jackie Kennedy told her new press secretary, Pamela Turnure, in 1961. Jackie was mobbed by reporters. What she wore, what she did, and how she raised her children became a source of public fascination. This is

Eleanor Roosevelt addresses a meeting of the National Women's Committee of Mobilization for Human Needs to publicize a matter she felt was important.

why she became the first presidential wife to hire her own press secretary. Although Pam Turnure worked in the East Wing, all her press releases were issued by her boss, Pierre Salinger—John Kennedy's press secretary. Even so, there were occasions when statements made by the two press secretaries conflicted. For example, while Turnure was denying a rumor that the Kennedys were going to build a home in Virginia, Salinger was confirming it.

Like Eleanor Roosevelt, Jackie was raised in an aristocratic family and had servants to carry out her wishes, but she did not share Eleanor's interest in politics, preferring to raise her young children and devote herself to cultural and artistic projects. Unlike her immediate predecessors, Jackie hired a large staff to help her meet her obligations, forty people in all, including clerks and messengers. She chose to recruit experts and supervise them rather than take a hands-on approach herself. To guide them, she wrote lengthy memos, scrawled in longhand. Social secretary Letitia Baldrige acted as her chief of staff. She directed the East Wingers and answered directly to Jackie for their actions. The First Lady paid attention to details, and little that interested her escaped her notice.

The First Lady shied away from the constantly ringing phones and interruptions of East Wing staffers and maintained her own office in the Treaty Room of the White House, reading and commenting on folders they sent her concerning her projects, speeches, correspondence, and schedule. Her own correspondence division handled the daily mail, which averaged over 200 letters a day during her first year.[5] She received a sampling of the mail and answered the most touching herself, forwarding many pleas for assistance to the appropriate government agency.

Relationships between members of the East and West Wings were not always smooth. Baldrige described it as a "civil war . . . based on nothing less than sex. Our male colleagues would walk all over us unless we fought back."[6] At issue was who would make decisions, such as scheduling appearances, for the First Lady. One sign of the tension between the two staffs was anticipated as early as Inauguration Day, when Baldrige swapped typewriters between the East and West Wings, leaving the men with the older, inferior models intended for the women. The problem was symbolic of the difficulties women faced in achieving equality with men.

The tensions between East and West Wings diminished but did not disappear when Lady Bird Johnson became First Lady in 1963. A West Wing advisor canceled the delivery of newspapers to the East Wing, but the service was resumed after the First Lady's staff put up a fight. Lady Bird transformed the East Wing into an efficient organization capable of making the traditional social duties of a First Lady serve her husband's political goals. As a politician's wife who successfully managed the family's radio station, she approached the East Wing from the perspective of a corporate businesswoman and made it run more efficiently. Instead of relying on handwritten memos, she stayed in touch with the staff by telephone, calling them hourly because she preferred her privacy and worked in her bedroom. She did not involve herself with flower arrangements or menus, leaving those to the staff, so she could concentrate on the issues facing her husband. Members of the president's staff briefed her and kept her up to date.

To serve as her press secretary and staff director, she appointed Liz Carpenter, an experienced newspaperwoman who also drafted many of her speeches. In the press division were six full-time employees, while four others took over social duties under the direction of social secretary Bess Abell. Two employees managed the First Lady's beautification project, and four took care of the mail. Letters to the First Lady arrived in droves, 3,500 during the last week in January 1965, for example. Lady Bird realized how important letters written in her name were to the people who received them. She urged her staff to use the dictionary, telling them, "Let's make these letters glow. I see them framed in hotels— from First Ladies and Presidents, and I want mine not to have any grammatical errors. I want them to be ones I'm proud of."[7] When she needed more staff she borrowed them temporarily from the West Wing. She was able to reshape the Office of First Lady because she did not get bogged down in details, delegated responsibility to others, and most important, because her husband supported her efforts to help him and even used her press secretary on occasion to write jokes into his speeches.

Her successor, Pat Nixon, became First Lady in 1969. She was a self-sufficient woman who had to learn how to utilize her staff and not try to do everything herself. For example, she spent four hours a day reading, and sometimes personally responding to, the 1,500 or so letters addressed to her because they gave her personal contact with the public. She refused to use an autopen and personally signed all letters that went out in her name as well as autograph cards. She told Gwen King, who was in charge of her correspondence, to help needy letter writers by referring them to government agencies. Like Eleanor Roosevelt, she personally handled the most desperate cases. When asked why she spent so much time on this task, she replied, "When a letter from the White House arrives in a small town, it's shown to all the neighbors, and often published in the local paper. It's very important to the people who receive it."[8]

In addition to a social secretary and press secretary, Pat had eight assistants to handle arrangements for trips, deal with correspondence, and handle special projects. She heeded Lady Bird's advice and set up her own office in a dressing room off her bedroom, receiving phone calls and notes from her staff which she answered promptly. She was close to her staff, was willing to discuss their personal problems with them, and gave them gifts to reward their efforts. She even trapped flies for the pet frog of a staff member's daughter. In return, they gave her their loyalty, but this was no guarantee that they would keep their jobs.

Pat had selected Gerry van der Heuvel as her press secretary, but before the year was out, H. R. Haldeman, President Nixon's chief of staff, removed her. Pat placed her in a job at the State Department. Haldeman and Pat picked Connie Stuart as the new press secretary after the First Lady made it clear that a male press director would be unacceptable to her and to the ladies of the press. Dissatisfied with Stuart's performance, Haldeman ousted her, too, and assistant press secretary Helen Smith took over. Despite the personnel changes, Pat succeeded in revealing little about her feelings or political knowledge to reporters although, like her predecessors, she made herself accessible to them.

Haldeman tried to dominate the East Wing. He often interfered in its operations, complaining about the food served at receptions and even suggesting performers to entertain at the White House. He and other presidential assistants in the West Wing saw that the president did not treat his wife as a political partner except when he was campaigning. Accordingly, they minimized her role in his administration. Possibly, members of the West Wing also feared that a powerful First Lady would undermine their influence over the president, so they did their best to keep her in the background. For example, Smith wrote, "Many times we would receive staff memos from Haldeman informing us that the President was about to go somewhere and we would see that the First Lady was not included."[9] When she was joining her husband on a trip, her staff was told at the last minute, making it difficult for them to prepare a schedule of appearances for her. Earlier, Connie Stuart had called Haldeman to task in a memo, suggesting that "the spirit of detente and cooperation between the President's staff and Mrs. Nixon's staff seems to be sagging a bit."[10] The First Lady's personal appearances and trips were mostly designed to get her out of the way, yet she was a popular and capable woman.

What had happened was that her husband chose to isolate himself to work on matters of policy and left the day-to-day running of the government to his chief of staff and other aides. The president did not know how poorly his wife was treated, and she chose not to complain to him about all the slights she received, only bringing matters that truly concerned her to his attention. If she wanted to go on a trip, she told him. She had always been a submissive wife, putting her husband's interests before her own, and confrontation was not her style. East Wing staffers observed that when Pat gave an order to a member of the West Wing, it was usually ignored, but orders relating to her that came from the president were promptly obeyed. She had other methods for dealing with the West Wing. In one case, when Haldeman failed to consult her and ordered bleacher type seats for the East Room that offended her taste, she simply did not use them. As a result of her refusal to challenge her husbands' aides and assert her own independence, the East Wing gradually became an adjunct of the West Wing, rather than an equal operation.

Adopting her husband's policy of candor and honesty in government, in 1974 Betty Ford became a more outspoken and active First Lady than her predecessor. Gerald Ford supported her activities, and this gave her some power as well as responsibilities. When the president's chief of staff, Donald Rumsfeld, urged him to cut some of his wife's staff as an economy measure, Ford told him to take it up directly with his wife, and few changes were made.

Betty had about twenty-eight people working for her in the East Wing, but she wanted more. She kept many of Pat's aides but replaced the social secretary first with Nancy Ruwe and then with Maria

Downs, so that things would be done her way. Sheila Weidenfeld served as press secretary and was the first member of the East Wing to attend the presidential press secretary's daily staff meetings, which helped improve relations between the two staffs. Betty held regular weekly meetings with the East Wing staff to stay on top of their work. Flooded with 50,000 pieces of mail after her breast cancer surgery, Betty relied on her staff and volunteers to acknowledge the letters and donations with a printed card.

The president's confidence in his wife did not always carry over to the West Wing. They still treated members of the East Wing like second-class citizens. Equipment was still a problem, and Press Secretary Weidenfeld had difficulty securing wire-service machines for her office. One of the First Lady's aides, who prepared news summaries, resigned because she was paid less than her male equivalent on the president's staff. Betty, herself, admitted that she did not always get along with her husband's chief assistant, Robert Hartmann, because he tried to control the president's life. If she felt that she or her staff was mistreated, she acted. In one case, when the National Security Council and State Department were preparing for Queen Elizabeth's visit, she phoned the chief of the National Security Council, telling him, "General, I want this visit to be completely handled by my staff, so would you please name someone from your staff for us to have as liaison with the State Department."[11] In another instance, Betty, an advocate of equal rights for women, presented a West Winger with a "male chauvinist pig" tie.

In 1977, when she became First Lady, Rosalynn Carter pressured her husband, Jimmy, to increase her staff, but he resisted, explaining, "Everybody always wants more staff, and that's why the federal government gets so overloaded."[12] The East Wing was reorganized, and as a result, Rosalynn herself had to personalize and autograph photographs, cards, and other items, but often she relied on the autopen when dealing with numerous requests from school classes. During her first fourteen months as First Lady, she received 152,000 letters and signed 150 photographs a week.[13]

Rosalynn decided to break with tradition and establish her own office in the East Wing. "I wanted our [living] quarters to be home, a place to escape from the work and the staff."[14] She held weekly meetings with her staff. Mary Hoyt was press secretary, charged with making sure that East Wing press releases meshed with the West

Wing's. The press office now conducted research as well. Projects divisions established community liaisons. The heavy workload in the newly christened Office of the First Lady demanded an official chief of staff, so Rosalynn hired Kit Dobelle to direct East Wing operations and its twenty-one employees. Kit also attended briefings of the senior West Wing staff and was paid the same amount as presidential chief of staff Hamilton Jordan. As social secretary, Rosalynn chose Gretchen Poston, a friend of Vice President Walter Mondale's wife, Joan. In 1977, Rosalynn boosted the salaries of her aides, the highest receiving $45,000; two were paid $40,000; seven got between $20,000 and $40,000; while eight got less than 20,000."[15]

East Wing operations became more important, reflecting the power Rosalynn exercised as her husband's partner in politics and policy. Not since Lady Bird Johnson had the staff been so well integrated into the president's administration. Rosalynn received briefings from the president's domestic and national security staffs and voiced strong opinions of her own that were respected by those who heard them. She worked in cooperation with her husband's staff, but staffers in the Office of First Lady still had occasional difficulties with their West Wing counterparts, reflecting lingering male chauvinism as well as a lack of daily personal communication and interaction, because the two staffs were headquartered in different parts of the White House.

As First Lady from 1981–1989, Nancy Reagan could have made the Office of First Lady an important part of her husband's presidency, as her predecessors Lady Bird Johnson and Rosalynn Carter had done. She could even benefit from a new law passed in 1978 that separated East Wing funding from the general budget for the White House and gave her $650,000 a year for East Wing operations. Unfortunately, Nancy did not make the most of her opportunities. She went through three speechwriters, three social secretaries, three project directors, three press secretaries, and five chiefs of staff.[16] Some believed that her perfectionism, her obsessive concern for her husband's image, and her worries about her own popularity led to the frequent changes in personnel.

She had sixteen staffers to help her fulfill her duties. Senior staff members met three times a week to schedule events and deal with issues.[17] As their predecessors had done, they helped her with the mail, passing on letters requesting help to government agencies. In

Nancy Reagan was very concerned about the public's image of her husband's administration.

1981, she received 78,803 letters, and by 1987 the number had risen to 85,930, mostly relating to drug-abuse matters and personal appeals for help.[18] Her staff also drafted her speeches, tried to create favorable treatment of her in the press, researched and managed her projects, and assisted her in planning and carrying out White House entertaining.

Her chiefs of staff were men who attended staff briefings by the president's chief of staff because of the First Lady's interest in politics, her husband's schedule, and issues such as drugs. This should have encouraged cooperation and coordination between the East and West Wing, but it did not. Staffers in the Office of the First Lady were not invited to a senior staff Christmas party, although women working in the West Wing were included. They were also denied tennis privileges and had to share quarters during trips while West Wingers were assigned single rooms.

Nancy did little to build their morale. When they could not supply her with the details she demanded, she went over their heads and consulted with the president's deputy chief of staff, Michael Deaver. Preferring masculine advice, she unintentionally fueled the war between the sexes by not defending her staff or looking to them for advice. What's more, she located her office outside the East Wing, on the second floor in the center of the White House, halfway between the East and West Wings. She used the phone to communicate with the president's staff and her own, determined to protect the power and influence of the president from all who would use him to their own advantage. "When I die, I'm going to have a phone in one hand and my phone book in the other," she said.[19]

When Ronald Reagan was ill with cancer (see Chapter 6), she became even more protective. She exercised so much power that staff members in both wings were afraid to cross her. Communications Director David Gergen admitted, "It would concern me a great deal to learn that she was unhappy with me."[20] When Donald Regan became President Reagan's chief of staff, he failed to realize how much power Nancy exerted and offended her by neglecting to return her calls, poorly preparing the president for press conferences, and by objecting to all the scheduling changes she demanded for her husband, upon the advice of her astrologer. In 1987, Nancy made sure that Regan lost his job (see Chapter 9).

It is difficult to judge the impact of First Lady Hillary Rodham Clinton on the Office of First Lady. She moved her office into the West Wing, demonstrating, even more openly than Rosalynn Carter had, that she was the president's political partner. Biographers and historians have not yet analyzed how this move affected the Office of First Lady or its relations with the West Wing, nor have they described Hillary's role in directing the East Wing staff. Her aides numbered only seventeen, plus volunteers, a demonstration of Bill Clinton's policy of downsizing the government. With Eleanor Roosevelt as her admitted role model and the experiences of powerful First Ladies Lady Bird Johnson, Rosalynn

Carter, and Nancy Reagan as examples, Hillary did not undertake her duties without guidance from the past.

Hillary and her successors will continue to shape the Office of First Lady and refine its mission. How they will reduce the rivalry between the East and West Wings remains to be seen. What is certain is that the Office of First Lady will change with each administration, reflecting the personality of the First Lady, her interests, and the power she derives from her relationship with her husband. Presidential wives have come a long way since the days of Eleanor Roosevelt, when just two women assisted the First Lady in carrying out the president's wishes and in fulfilling her personal commitment to public service.

Eleven

Making a Graceful Exit

*I never realized what a strain I was
under continuously until it was over.*

—Edith Roosevelt

In 1889, with the inauguration of President Benjamin Harrison, Grover Cleveland and his wife Frankie left the Executive Mansion, as was customary. As Frankie was being escorted to her waiting carriage, she told White House servant Jerry Smith, "Now, Jerry, I want you to take good care of all the furniture and ornaments in the house, and not let any of them get lost or broken, for I want to find everything just as it is now, when we come back again."[1] He asked her when she expected to return and to his great surprise heard her say, "We are coming back just four years from to-day."[2]

In 1893, she kept her word and moved back into the White House for four more years. With the inauguration of William McKinley in 1897, the Clevelands had to leave the Executive Mansion for a second and final time. Looking forward to a quiet life, 33-year-old Frankie and her husband made plans to settle in Princeton, New Jersey. Before departing for the train station, she asked the domestic staff to assemble so that she could say goodbye to them. When she thanked them for their service to her, she started to cry. Frankie was very attached to the servants, remembering them on their birthdays and at Christmas with little gifts, and they adored her. By bidding them a formal farewell, Frankie started a tradition other First Ladies would follow.

While Frankie was the only First Lady to retire from the White House twice, on August 9, 1974, Pat Nixon became the only First Lady to leave the Executive Mansion as a result of a presidential resignation. Her husband had participated in a cover-up to protect his White House aides from FBI and congressional investigations into a June 1972 break-in at Democratic Party National Headquarters at the Watergate Complex, where eavesdropping equipment had been installed. His aides were guilty of other misconduct as well.

Pat did not know about her husband's involvement in the cover-up and loyally defended him to reporters, claiming, "I think it has been blown all out of proportion."[3] Over the next two years, they repeatedly questioned her about Watergate, but she ignored them. She even made a joke of it, explaining, "I just pretend I don't hear them. The next thing I know there will be the report that I'm getting deaf!"[4] Amid revelations of scandal that led directly to the White House, she carried on her duties as First Lady as usual. In July 1973, it was revealed that her husband had taped conversations about Watergate with his staff, but he refused to turn all these recordings over to legal authorities or Congress until the Supreme Court ordered him to comply in July 1974. "If they had been *my* tapes, I would have burned or destroyed them because they were like a private diary, not public property," Pat confided to a longtime friend.[5] As an attorney, Richard Nixon knew he could not destroy evidence needed in a criminal case against his White House aides without penalty.

Pat knew that the Judiciary Committee of the House of Representatives voted charges of impeachment against her husband on July 27–28, 1974, and were proceeding to remove him from office. Among other offenses, he was accused of obstructing justice and abusing the powers of the presidency. She was prepared to help him fight to reduce the charges and clear his name, but this was no longer acceptable to him. With the release of the incriminating tapes, his support in Congress eroded, and on August 2, he chose to resign rather than fight to stay in office. Pat learned of his decision from her daughter Julie. The president had failed to consult her during all his years in office and this occasion was no different.

Pat Nixon's agony is obvious as she watches her husband make his farewell speech.

Quietly, Pat began to pack the Nixon's possessions and important papers. She also canceled an order for new White House china that she had selected a few days earlier. Withdrawing from public appearances, she sorted out items to be sent to storage and others to be shipped to the Nixon home in San Clemente, California. On August 8, when the president delivered his speech to the nation announcing his decision, she watched him on television with other family members in the West Hall. He did not think he could get through the speech if they were in the Oval Office with him.

The next day, to protect her privacy, she wore dark glasses as she joined her husband to bid farewell to the White House domestic staff. Then the Nixon family proceeded to the East Room where the president spoke to members of the cabinet and his aides. Noticing the television cameras, Pat protested, "Oh, Dick, you can't have it televised," but he insisted.[6] She removed her sunglasses and bravely faced the cameras. Although he spoke warmly about his late mother, not once during his entire speech did her husband praise Pat Nixon. Perhaps if he had he would have been unable to continue, for he was well aware that he had let his family down. Then, incoming president Gerald Ford and his wife, Betty, escorted the Nixons to the waiting helicopter on the White House lawn. Pat turned to Betty and commented, "My heavens, they've even rolled out the red carpet for us, isn't that something? Well, Betty, you'll see many of these red carpets, and you'll get so you hate 'em."[7] As her sentiments might suggest, Pat always preferred private life to public life.

Pat remained in seclusion, gardening and reading in San Clemente, California. A few months after her husband's resignation, she nursed him through a life-threatening ailment. Then, in 1976, she suffered a stroke and worked hard to recover the use of her paralyzed left hand. In 1980, the Nixons moved to the East Coast to be closer to their grandchildren, settling first in New York and then in New Jersey. She had a minor stroke in 1983. While her husband eventually became respected as an elder statesman, consulted by presidents, Pat enjoyed her life as a private citizen, shopping and taking her grandchildren for excursions until her death from lung cancer in 1993.

Most First Ladies felt sad when their husbands left office, but few had regrets. Martha Washington wrote, "The General and I feel like children just released from school or from a hard taskmaster."[8] In a similar fashion, Edith Roosevelt admitted, "I never realized what a strain I was under continuously until it was over."[9] Some wives, however, would have liked to stay on as First Ladies but had to leave when their husbands were defeated at election time. Abigail Adams wrote, "I can truly and from my heart say that the most mortifying circumstance attendant upon my retirement from public Life is, that my power of doing good to my fellow creatures is curtailed and diminished."[10] Rosalynn Carter had a different reason for wanting to remain First Lady. She confessed, "I miss the world of politics. . . . [O]ur loss at the polls is the biggest single reason I'd like to be back in the White House. I don't like to lose."[11]

Putting partisanship aside, presidential wives have graciously made their successors welcome at the White House, showing them the public rooms and private quarters, and answering questions about life in the Executive Mansion. Democrats Frankie and Grover Cleveland even hosted a private White House dinner for the Republican Harrisons before the inauguration of Benjamin Harrison in 1889. Since 1968, transitions between presidential administrations have become smoother, with funding and staff made available by law to help an incoming president handle the transfer of power in an orderly manner. The role of presidents' wives, however, in showing their successors through the White House still depends on custom, as does their practice of riding beside the incoming First Lady to the Capitol for the swearing-in ceremonies. Edith Wilson and Florence Harding started this tradition in 1921. Modern First Ladies have accepted their retirement with dignity. In doing so, they have set an example for other women whose husbands have had to step down from positions or jobs they once held.

Paying the Ultimate Price

Eight presidents have died in office, four from illness or natural causes and four by assassination (see Appendix). Most First Ladies have been role models of dignity and courage when they unexpectedly became widows, but Mary Lincoln could not cope with her loss. She was the first presidential wife to lose her husband to an assassin's bullet. On April 14, 1865, she sat beside Abraham Lincoln at Ford's Theater, watching *Our American Cousin*, when actor John Wilkes Booth, a Confederacy sympathizer, shot him. While keeping vigil at Petersen House where her husband lay dying, she collapsed and was brought back to the White House. In keeping with tradition, she did not attend the services for her husband. The funeral was arranged by her son Robert. He escorted the president's body to Springfield, Illinois, for burial. The funeral train stopped at a number of cities along the way so people could pay their respects to the slain leader. In New York City, one of the train stops, 3-year-old Edith Kermit, and her future husband, $6\frac{1}{2}$ year old Theodore Roosevelt, looked out a window to watch the funeral procession.

Bereft and unstable, Mary defied most nineteenth-century mourning rituals. She was expected to wear black clothing for two years, but she continued to do so for the rest of her life. Contrary to custom, she refused to receive condolence callers. She simply took to her bed and remained there until May 23, 1865. When Mary finally left the Executive Mansion, she was accused of removing government property. Unsupervised, the White House servants and curiosity seekers had stolen much of the china and silver while she was bedridden. Her behavior became so erratic that from May 1875 to September 1876, she was confined in a mental hospital.

Unlike Mary Lincoln, Crete Garfield won the nation's admiration and respect for her devotion to her dying husband. On July 2, 1881, James Garfield had been about to board a train for the New Jersey seashore, where his wife was recuperating from malaria, when disappointed office-seeker Charles J. Guiteau shot him. Crete rushed back to the White House and stayed by her husband's bedside, faithfully nursing him throughout the hot and muggy Washington summer. In September, it was decided to move him to the seashore, where he died on September 19. Crete was the first presidential wife to participate in the funeral services for her husband. She made sure that the public could see her as she rode the train taking his remains back to his home state of Ohio for burial. The American people were so touched by her selfless conduct that they voluntarily raised $360,000 to benefit her and her five children.

Jackie Kennedy's conduct inspired the nation after her husband was shot by Lee Harvey Oswald on November 22, 1963, as the Kennedys were riding in a motorcade through Dallas, Texas. Wearing a bloodstained pink suit, the thirty-four-year-old widow witnessed Lyndon Johnson's swearing-in as president aboard *Air Force One* shortly after her husband was pronounced dead. In Washington, she carefully orchestrated arrangements for John's funeral, duplicating the rituals and mourning decorations used to honor Abraham Lincoln. She and her children participated in the ceremonies and watched John Kennedy being laid to rest at Arlington National Cemetery. Her dignity and composure endeared her to the public watching the ceremonies on television.

JUST REWARDS

The widows of presidents and former presidents have received certain benefits from the government. Congress granted Martha Washington and her widowed successors the right to apply for the franking privilege, enabling them to mail letters free of charge by simply signing their names in place of stamps. Twenty First Ladies have used it.[12] The lawmakers also have made financial provisions for widows. Congress purchased James Madison's presidential papers from Dolley Madison to help her meet expenses. Unfortunately, her wastrel son from a previous marriage, Payne Todd, squandered the money, so the lawmakers came to Dolley's rescue again by buying a second set of documents but placing the money in trust so that her son could not get his hands on it.

Mary Lincoln, shown here in mourning clothing, was almost in poverty before Congress voted her a pension.

In 1841, Congress began awarding pensions on an individual basis to former First Ladies, starting with Anna Harrison, whose husband died in office. She received a single payment, the equivalent of his salary for one year because he was president for only one month before he died. Julia Tyler had more difficulty wresting funds from Congress. She had sided with the South during the Civil War, and her husband had served in the Confederate government. Her pleas for financial help were ignored until 1882, when she was granted a yearly pension of $5,000.

Mary Lincoln felt she deserved a generous pension because her husband had been assassinated. Abraham Lincoln left her $35,000, but she was always insecure about money and even traveled to New York to raise money by selling her clothing. The sale was a failure, and she was widely criticized. She sailed to Europe, where she could live more cheaply but returned in 1870 when Congress voted her a pension of $3,000 a year. That sum was raised to $5,000 in 1882, just before her death. Crete Garfield and Sarah Polk were given similar sums. When Edith Roosevelt was widowed in 1919, she wanted to turn down the money because she was independently wealthy, but she was encouraged to accept it lest Congress deny aid to future presidential widows who might need it. Jackie Kennedy received a pension of $50,000. In addition to financial support, secret service protection was extended to former presidential couples after the assassination of John F. Kennedy in 1963.

First Ladies' adjustment to private life was as individual and as varied as their own personalities and circumstances. Three presidential wives—Letitia Tyler, Caroline Harrison, and Ellen Wilson—never faced such challenges because they died in the White House, and a fourth, Abigail Fillmore, passed away just three weeks after her husband left office. For the most part, nineteenth-century First Ladies led quiet, retiring lives in their home states and when widowed, spent their time preserving their husband's memory. Of course, there were some exceptions. Upon James Madison's death in 1836, Dolley moved back to Washington, where her splendid parties made her the nation's unofficial hostess. Congress voted her a unique honor: when she attended their sessions, she was to be escorted to a seat on the floor of the House of Representatives instead of sitting in the Visitors' Gallery, as was customary. She willingly advised and supported her successors as First Lady, continuing a tradition begun by Martha Washington that persists to this day. Southern Democrat Julia Tyler also returned to the Capitol after the Civil War, when she was pressuring Congress for a pension, and managed to secure government jobs for her children from Republican administrations.

Julia Grant had time to reflect on her life while she nursed her husband when he developed cancer in 1884. After his death in 1885, she became the first presidential widow to pen her own memoirs. They were "a panacea for loneliness, a tonic for old age."[13] Most of the book chronicled her experiences on the Grants' worldwide tour instead of focusing on their family life or politics. The memoirs were not published during her lifetime, but they established a trend for her twentieth-century successors. Among the wives who became authors of autobiographies or other books were Caroline Harrison, Lou Hoover, Grace Coolidge, Jackie Kennedy, Edith Roosevelt, Nellie Taft,

Edith Wilson, Eleanor Roosevelt, Lady Bird Johnson, Betty Ford, Rosalynn Carter, Nancy Reagan, and Barbara Bush. Eleanor Roosevelt continued her newspaper column until shortly before her death.

Four years after her husband died in 1908, Frankie Cleveland became the first presidential widow to remarry. She wed Thomas J. Preston, Jr., a Princeton University professor, thereby setting a precedent for a twentieth-century presidential widow, Jackie Kennedy. She married Greek shipping tycoon Aristotle Onassis in 1968, after the assassination of her brother-in-law Robert F. Kennedy. Both women had young children to raise and protect from the curious public.

Some twentieth-century former First Ladies followed the example of their nineteenth-century counterparts by traveling or nursing their ailing husbands. For example, Edith Roosevelt, Grace Coolidge, and Bess Truman traveled abroad with their husbands or on their own. Edith Wilson, Mamie Eisenhower, and Nancy Reagan faithfully cared for their ailing husbands. Woodrow Wilson never fully recovered from his stroke; Ike had a very weak heart, and Ronald Reagan developed Alzheimer's disease, the gradual deterioration of the memory and other mental functions. After her husband died in 1969, Mamie Eisenhower became more outspoken, although she preferred her more traditional role as a wife and mother in comparison with feminists, who worked in addition to running households and rearing children. She even delivered a talk to the graduating class of Gettysburg College, near the farm where she and Ike had retired after they left the White House.

Twentieth-century former First Ladies also charted new paths as opportunities for women expanded. Some even went to work. After Calvin Coolidge's death in 1933, Grace became the head of the Clark School for the Deaf, where she had trained as a teacher when she was a young woman. In 1946, a year after Franklin died, Eleanor Roosevelt received an appointment from his successor, Harry Truman, to serve as a delegate to the United Nations. As the conscience of the world, she was instrumental in securing passage of the Universal Declaration of Human Rights in 1948. After Onassis's death in 1975, Jackie Kennedy took a job. She became an editor, first at Viking Press and then at Doubleday.

Other wives of former presidents continued to support causes they had sponsored when they lived in the White House. Lou Hoover kept up her ties to the Girl Scouts and was active in the

Salvation Army. Eleanor continued to speak on behalf of civil rights for African-Americans and greater opportunities for women. Jackie Kennedy's interest in historic preservation extended to participating in the successful campaign to save New York City's Grand Central Station from being torn down. She also appeared at fundraisers and social events in support of the arts. Like Bess Truman before her and most of her successors, she was involved in the project to house her husband's papers in a presidential library.

In 1982, nine years after her husband died, Lady Bird Johnson founded the privately funded National Wildflower Research Center in Austin, Texas, to encourage the planting and preservation of the country's natural floral heritage. Suffering from a pinched nerve and arthritis, Betty Ford relied on painkillers as First Lady. After leaving the White House, she also suffered from depression and alcoholism. In 1978 she entered a treatment program and then put her experience to good use when she founded the Betty Ford Center for Drug and Alcohol Rehabilitation at Rancho Mirage, California. Rosalynn Carter kept occupied writing books on aging and working alongside her husband as a volunteer at Habitat for Humanity, building low-cost housing for the needy. Nancy Reagan chose to head her own foundation to provide funds for drug-prevention programs and drug-awareness education. Barbara Bush continued to support literacy programs.

Some former First Ladies became involved in politics. In 1932, Edith Roosevelt, not known for taking a position in public or giving speeches, addressed a large rally of the Republican faithful at Madison Square Garden, declaring her preference for Herbert Hoover to her late husband's cousin Franklin for president. Edith believed that Franklin's programs would destroy American liberty and individualism.

It was no surprise that Eleanor Roosevelt was active in politics after she left the White House. She worked on behalf of such liberal Democratic candidates as Governor Adlai Stevenson of Illinois and Congressman Edward I. Koch of New York. After Harry Truman died in 1972, his widow Bess became the honorary cochairperson of Thomas Eagleton's senatorial reelection campaign in 1974, along with her idol, baseball great Stan Musial. In 1976 she supported State Senator Ike Skelton, who won a seat in Congress. Bess died at age ninety-seven in 1982, living longer than any other First Lady. Barbara Bush, who avoided political controversies during her husband's presidency, campaigned actively for the Bush's son, George, much as she had for his father, and celebrated when he became governor of Texas in 1995.

Many First Ladies have made significant contributions to the nation while they occupied the White House and after they became private citizens. Their achievements have both reflected and expanded expectations of what American women can and should do. From hostesses and fashion plates, they have emerged as politicians, policy makers, and diplomats with offices of their own to supervise. At the same time, they have continued to raise children, manage the Executive Mansion, and cherish their husbands. Who says they can't have it all?

Changing Expectations for the Future

With the arrival of the twenty-first century, however, Americans may want to review the role First Ladies play in society and government. Presidential wives may continue to choose the tasks they feel most capable of performing, much as they have done in the past. Alternatively, their ever-increasing duties may be legally defined and limited since the women are actually unelected, unpaid volunteers, accountable only to their husbands. Should they be trusted with so much responsibility? Should they be given even more? Can they handle the workload or do they need more assistance? Do they have too much power or too little?

In the future, more First Ladies will probably have professional commitments of their own that they may not wish to abandon while their husbands are president. Problems with potential conflicts of interest between a First Lady's job and her husband's position may have to be resolved by law. This has already been done with presidential couples' investments and businesses. These are managed by professionals and only returned to the First Family's control after they leave office.

If First Ladies pursue their own careers, in all likelihood, their staffs will have to take on even more functions. As one example, the social secretary may assume more formal hostessing duties. White House guests, however, will probably feel snubbed if they are not greeted and entertained by the First Lady. If presidential wives rely on their staffs to fill in for them, it will be all the more

A proud legacy: six of America's First Ladies gather together.

important for them to develop methods to better coordinate East and West Wing personnel and end their rivalry.

Perhaps, twenty-first-century Americans will decide to pay First Ladies for their service to the nation. In 1946, Representative James G. Fulton, a Pennsylvania Republican, raised the issue in Congress, but nothing was done. Both Betty Ford and Rosalynn Carter endorsed the idea, but traditionally, the public has held that a president's salary includes his wife's activities. This is the prevailing practice in corporations and even churches. It comes from the legal doctrine that a husband and wife are one person under the law. Whether a change is desirable or possible remains to be seen.

Just as no one in the nineteenth century might have anticipated that twentieth-century First Ladies would serve as envoys to Latin America or lead a task force to reorganize health care, no one today can predict what demands may be made of a president's partner in the decades to come. In her 1990 commencement speech at Wellesley College, Barbara Bush commented, "Somewhere out in this audience may even be someone who will one day follow in my footsteps, and preside over the White House as the president's spouse. I wish him well!"[14]

CHAPTER NOTES

Chapter One

1 Pamela Killian. *Barbara Bush: A Biography* (New York: St. Martin's Press, 1992), p. 10.

2 Ibid., p. 11.

3 Barbara Bush. *A Memoir* (New York: Charles Scribner's Sons, 1994), p. 337.

4 Ibid., Appendix C, p. 540.

5 Ibid.

6 Michael Kramer. "The Political Interest: It's Not Going to Be Pretty," *Time*, 139, (April 20, 1992), p. 46.

7 Norman King. *The Woman in the White House: The Remarkable Story of Hillary Rodham Clinton* (New York: Carol Publishing Group, 1996), p. 156.

8 Ibid., p. 157.

9 Peter Hay. *All the Presidents' Ladies: Anecdotes of the Women Behind the Men in the White House* (New York: Penguin Books, 1989), pp. 144–145.

10 King, p. 165.

11 Joseph P. Lash. *Eleanor and Franklin: The Story of Their Relationship Based on Eleanor Roosevelt's Private Papers* (New York: W. W. Norton, 1971), p. 355.

12 Blanche Wiesen Cook. *Eleanor Roosevelt* 2 vols. (New York: Penguin Books, 1992), vol. 1, p. 474.

13 Carl Sferrazza Anthony. *First Ladies: The Saga of the Presidents' Wives and Their Power* 2 vols. (New York: Quill/William Morrow, 1990), vol. 1, p. 42.

14 Nancy Tuckerman. *"Reminiscence,"* The Estate of Jacqueline Kennedy Onassis (New York: Sotheby's, 1996), p. 21.

15 Paul F. Boller. *Presidential Wives: An Anecdotal History* (New York: Oxford University Press, 1988), p. 131.

16 Betty Boyd Caroli. *First Ladies* (New York: Oxford University Press, 1995) p. 155.

17 Ibid., p. 210.

18 Marian Means. *The Woman in the White House: The Lives, Times, and Influence of Twelve Notable First Ladies* (New York: Random House, 1963), p. 227.

19 Anthony, vol. 1, p. 126.

20 Ibid., vol. 1, p. 210.

21 Hay, p. 182.

22 Nancy Skarmeas. *First Ladies of the White House* (Nashville: Ideals Publications, Inc., 1995), p.73.

23 Caroli, p. xxi.

Chapter Two

1 Carl Sferrazza Anthony. *First Ladies: The Saga of the Presidents' Wives and Their Power* 2 vols. (New York: Quill/William Morrow, 1990), vol. 1, p. 260.

2 Irwin "Ike" Hoover. *Forty-two Years in the White House* (Boston: Houghton Mifflin, 1934), p. 303.

3 Paul F. Boller, Jr. *Presidential Wives: An Anecdotal History* (New York: Oxford University Press, 1988), pp. 282-283.

4 Ibid., p. 283.

5 Marianne Means, *The Woman in the White House: The Lives, Times, and Influence of Twelve Notable First Ladies* (New York: Random House, 1965), p. 11.

6 Bess Furman, *White House Profile: A Social History of the White House, Its Occupants and its Festivities* (Boston: Bobbs-Merrill Company, Inc., 1951), p. 31.

7 Means, p. 69.

8 Webb Garrison, *A Treasury of White House Tales* (Nashville: Rutledge Hill Press, 1989), p. 111.

9 Nancy Skarmeas, *First Ladies of the White House* (Nashville: Ideals Publications, 1995), p. 13.

10 Skarmeas, p. 21.

11 Caroli, p. 93.

12 Garrison, p. 191.

13 Joseph P. Lash, *Franklin and Eleanor: The Story of Their Relationship, Based on Eleanor Roosevelt's Personal Papers* (New York: W. W. Norton & Company, Inc., 1971), p. 613.

14 Margaret Truman. *Bess W. Truman* (New York: Jove Books, 1987), p. 340.

15 Margaret Truman. *First Ladies* (New York: Random House, 1995), p. 216.

16 J.B. West, *Upstairs at the White House: My Life with the First Ladies* (New York: Coward, McCann & Geoghagen, 1973), p. 341.

17 Truman, *First Ladies*, p. 39.

18 West, p. 310.

19 Julie Nixon Eisenhower. *Pat Nixon* (New York: Zebra Books, 1986), p. 428.

20 Anthony, vol. 2, p. 280.

21 Donnie Radcliffe. *Hillary Rodham Clinton: A First Lady for Our Time* (New York: Warner Books, 1993), p. 250.

Chapter Three

1 Jean H. Baker, *Mary Todd Lincoln: A Biography* (New York: W. W. Norton, 1987), p. 235.

2 Ibid., p. 196.

3 Betty Boyd Caroli, *First Ladies* (New York: Oxford University Press, 1995), pp. 72–73.

4 Carl Sferrazza Anthony, *First Ladies: The Saga of the Presidents' Wives and Their Power,* 2 vols. (New York: Quill/William Morrow, 1990), vol. 1, p. 193.

5 Kitty Kelley, *Nancy Reagan: The Unauthorized Biography* (New York: Pocket Books, 1991), p. 309.

6 Paul F. Boller, Jr., *Presidential Wives: An Anecdotal History* (New York: Oxford University Press, 1988), p. 451.

7 Kelley, p. 385.

8 This paragraph is drawn from material found in Caroli, pp. 312–317.

9 J. B. West, *Upstairs at the White House: My Life with the First Ladies* (New York: Coward, McCann & Geoghegan, 1973), p. 59.

10 Margaret Truman, *First Ladies* (New York: Random House, 1995), p. 31.

11 Ibid., p. 38.

12 Donnie Radcliffe, *Simply Barbara Bush: A Portrait of America's Candid First Lady* (New York: Warner Books, 1989), p. 13.

13 Truman, p. 327.

14 Edith P. Mayo and Denise D. Meringolo, *First Ladies: Political Role and Public Image* (Washington, D.C. : Smithsonian Institution, 1994), p. 7.

Chapter Four

1 Haynes Johnson, *The Working White House* (New York: Praeger Publishers, 1975), p. 12.

2 Sylvia Jukes Morris, *Edith Kermit Roosevelt: Portrait of a First Lady* (New York: Coward, McCann & Geoghegan, 1980), p. 222.

3 Bess Furman, *White House Profile: A Social History of the White House, Its Occupants, and Its Festivities* (Boston: the Bobbs-Merrill Company, 1951), pp. 250–251.

4 Ibid., p. 334.

5 Johnson, p. 17.

6 J. B. West, *Upstairs at the White House: My Life with the First Ladies* (New York: Coward, McCann & Geoghegan,1973), p. 121.

7 Margaret Truman, *First Ladies* (New York: Random House, 1995), p. 158.

8 Lillian Rogers Parks, *My Thirty Years Backstairs at the White House* (New York: Fleet Publishing, 1961), p. 125.

9 Paul F. Boller, Jr. *Presidential Wives: An Anecdotal History* (New York: Oxford University Press, 1988), p. 296.

10 West, p. 77.

11 Ibid., p. 283.

Chapter Five

1 Rosalynn Carter, *First Lady from Plains* (Boston: Houghton Mifflin, 1984), p. 155.

2 Margaret Truman, *First Ladies* (New York: Random House, 1995), p. 8.

3 Julia Dent Grant, *The Personal Memoirs of Julia Dent Grant.* ed. John Y. Simon (New York: G.P. Putnam's Sons, 1975), p. 175.

4 Sylvia Jukes Morris, *Edith Kermit Roosevelt: Portrait of a First Lady* (New York: Coward, McCann & Geoghegan, 1980), p. 319.

5 Ibid., p. 268.

6 Paul F. Boller, Jr., *Presidential Wives: An Anecdotal History* (New York: Oxford University Press, 1988), p. 365.

7 Peter Hay, *All the Presidents' Ladies* (New York: Penguin Books, 1988), p. 134.

8 Jean H. Baker, *Mary Todd Lincoln: A Biography* (New York: W. W. Norton, 1987), p. 210.

9 Ishbel Ross, *Grace Coolidge and Her Era* (New York: Dodd, Mead, 1962), p. 123.

10 Ibid., p. 125.

11 Lillian Rogers Parks, *My Thirty Years Backstairs at the White House* (New York: Fleet Publishing, 1961), p. 249.

12 Marianne Means, *The Women in the White House: The Lives, Times, and Influence of Twelve Notable First Ladies* (New York: Random House, 1963), p. 14.

13 J. B. West, *Upstairs at the White House: My Life with the First Ladies* (New York: Coward, McCann & Geoghegan, 1973), p. 163.

14 Barbara Bush, *A Memoir* (New York: Charles Scribner's Sons, 1994), p. 510.

15 Betty Boyd Caroli, *First Ladies* (New York: Oxford University Press, 1995), p. 353.

Chapter Six

1 Feerick, John D., *From Failing Hands: The Story of Presidential Succession* (New York: Fordham University Press, 1965), p. 167.

2 Edith Bolling Wilson, *My Memoir* (Indianapolis: Bobbs-Merrill, 1938), p. 289.

3 Ibid.

4 Doris Kearns Goodwin, *No Ordinary Time: Franklin and Eleanor Roosevelt: The Home Front in World War II* (New York: Simon & Schuster, 1994), p. 503.

5 Joseph P. Lash, *Eleanor and Franklin: The Story of Their Relationship, Based on Eleanor Roosevelt's Private Papers* (New York: W. W. Norton, 1971), p. 695.

6 Carl Sferrazza Anthony, *First Ladies: The Saga of the Presidents' Wives and Their Power* 2 vols. (New York: Quill/William Morrow, 1990), vol. 1, 276–277.

7 Ibid., vol. 1, 277.

8 Ibid., vol. 2, p. 386.

9 Ibid.

10 Ibid., p. 582.

11 Feerick, p. 221.

12 Margaret Truman, *First Ladies* (New York: Random House, 1995), p. 13.

13 Morris, p. 294.

14 Lady Bird Johnson, *A White House Diary* (New York: Holt, Rinehart and Winston, 1970), p. 45.

Chapter Seven

1 Betty Boyd Caroli, *First Ladies* (New York: Oxford University Press, 1995), p. 21.

2 Ibid.

3 Joseph P. Lash, *Eleanor and Franklin: The Story of Their Relationship Based on Eleanor's Private Papers* (New York: W.W. Norton & Company, Inc., 1971), p. 623.

4 Ibid., p. 709.

5 Carl Sferrazza Anthony, *First Ladies: The Saga of the Presidents' Wives and Their Power* 2 vols. (New York: Quill/William Morrow, 1990), vol. 1, p. 384.

6 Edith Mayo and Denise Meringolo, *First Ladies: Political Role and Public Image* (Washington, D.C.: Smithsonian Institution, 1994), p. 34.

7 Ibid., p. 39.

8 Paul F. Boller, Jr., *Presidential Wives: An Anecdotal History* (New York: Oxford University Press, 1988), p. 408.

9 Pamela Killian, *Barbara Bush: A Biography* (New York: St. Martin's Press, 1992), p. 142.

10 Caroli, p. 221.

11 Anthony, vol. 1, p. 591.

12 Boller, p. 406.

13 Lady Bird Johnson, *A White House Diary* (New York: Holt, Rinehart and Winston, 1970), p. 198.

14 Anthony, vol. 2, p. 124.

15 Rosalynn Carter, *First Lady from Plains* (Boston: Houghton Mifflin, 1984), p. 117.

16 Donnie Radcliffe, *Hillary Rodham Clinton: First Lady for Our Time* (New York: Warner Books, 1993), p. 233.

17 U.S. Department of Commerce, *Bureau of the Census, Statistical Abstract of the United States 1994* (Washington, D.C.: Government Printing Office, 1994), p. 395.

Chapter Eight

1 Margaret Truman, *First Ladies* (New York: Random House, 1995), p. 55.

2 Joseph P. Lash, *Eleanor and Franklin: The Story of Their Relationship Based on Eleanor Roosevelt's Private Papers* (New York: W. W. Norton, 1971), p. 413.

3 Ibid., p. 532.

4 Edith P. Mayo and Denise D. Meringolo, *First Ladies: Political Role and Public Image* (Washington, D.C.: Smithsonian Institution, 1994), p. 24.

5 Carl Sferrazza Anthony, *First Ladies: The Saga of the Presidents' Wives and Their Power,* 2 vols. (New York: Quill/Morrow, 1990), vol. 1, p. 441.

6 Ibid., vol. 2, p. 27.

7 Paul F. Boller, Jr., *Presidential Wives: An Anecdotal History* (New York: Oxford University Press, 1988), p. 364.

8 Lady Bird Johnson, *A White House Diary* (New York: Holt, Rinehart and Winston, 1970), p. 271.

9 Anthony, vol. 2, p. 134.

10 Betty Ford, *The Times of My Life* (New York: Harper & Row, 1978), p. 201.

11 Rosalynn Carter, *First Lady From Plains* (Boston: Houghton Mifflin, 1984), p. 286.

Chapter Nine

1 Marianne Means, *The Woman in the White House: The Lives, Times, and Influence of Twelve Notable First Ladies* (New York: Random House, 1963), p. 81.

2 Margaret Truman, *First Ladies* (New York: Random House, 1995), p. 101.

3 Margaret Truman, *Bess W. Truman* (New York: Jove Books, 1987), pp. 322-323.

4 Means, p. 217.

5 J. B. West, *Upstairs at the White House: My Life with the First Ladies* (New York: Coward, McCann & Geoghegan, 1973), p. 78.

6 Doris Kearns Goodwin, *No Ordinary Time* New York: Simon & Schuster, 1994, p. 28.

7 John Sferrazza Anthony, *First Ladies: The Saga of the Presidents' Wives and Their Power* (New York: Quill/William Morrow, 1991), vol. 2, p. 276.

8 Truman, First Ladies, p. 322.

9 Norman King, *The Woman in the White House: The Remarkable Story of Hillary Rodham Clinton* (Carol Publishing Group, 1996), p. 200.

10 Betty Boyd Caroli, *First Ladies* (New York: Oxford University Press, 1995), p. 304.

11 Means, p. 91.

12 For a more complete, if not always objective, list of people Nancy forced out of the Reagan administration, see Kitty Kelley, *Nancy Reagan: The Unauthorized Biography* (New York: Pocket Star Books, 1991), pp. 355–357.

13 Means, p. 272.

14 Rosalynn Carter, *First Lady from Plains* (Boston: Houghton Mifflin, 1984), p. 194.

Chapter Ten

1 Betty Boyd Caroli, *First Ladies* (New York: Oxford University Press, 1995), p. 322.

2 Bess Furman, *Washington By-Line: A Personal History of a Newspaperwoman* (New York: Alfred A. Knopf, 1949), p. 194.

3 Carl Sferrazza Anthony, *First Ladies: The Saga of the Presidents' Wives and Their Power,* 2 vols. (New York: Quill/Morrow, 1990), vol. 1, p. 459.

4 C. David Heymann, *A Woman Named Jackie* (New York: Signet Books, 1990), p. 271.

5 Anthony, vol. 2, p. 49.

6 Ibid., p. 50.

7 Ibid., p. 113.

8 Paul F. Boller, Jr., *Presidential Wives: An Anecdotal History* (New York: Oxford University Press, 1988), p. 409.

9 Caroli, p. 250.

10 Julie Nixon Eisenhower, *Pat Nixon, The Untold Story* (New York: Zebra Books, 1986), p. 453.

11 Betty Ford, *The Times of My Life* (New York: Harper & Row, 1978), p. 224.

12 Rosalynn Carter, *First Lady from Plains* (Boston: Houghton Mifflin, 1984), p.168.

13 Ibid., p. 184.

14 Ibid., p. 151.

15 Webb Garrison, *A Treasury of White House Tales* (Nashville: Rutledge Hill Press, 1989), p. 160.

16 Anthony, vol. 2, p. 356.

17 Ibid., p. 357.

18 Nancy Kegan Smith and Mary C. Ryan, eds., *Modern First Ladies: Their Documentary Legacy* (Washington, D.C.: National Archives and Records Administration, 1989), p. 160.

19 Anthony, vol. 2, p. 369.

20 Ibid., p. 372.

Chapter Eleven

1 Paul F. Boller, Jr. *Presidential Wives: An Anecdotal History* (New York: Oxford University Press, 1988), p. 174.

2 Ibid.

3 Lester David, *The Lonely Lady of San Clemente* (New York: Thomas Y. Crowell, 1978), p. 167.

4 Julie Nixon Eisenhower, *Pat Nixon: The Untold Story* (New York: Zebra Books, 1986), pp. 637–638.

5 David, p. 163.

6 Eisenhower, p. 653.

7 Betty Ford, *The Times of My Life* (New York: Harper & Row, 1978), p. 3.

8 Boller, p. 7.

9 Sylvia Jukes Morris, *Edith Kermit Roosevelt: Portrait of a First Lady* (New York: Coward, McCann & Geoghegan, 1980), p. 349.

10 Carl Sferrazza Anthony, *First Ladies: The Saga of the Presidents' Wives and Their Power,* 2 vols. (New York: Quill/William Morrow, 1990), vol. 1, pp. 71-72.

11 Rosalynn Carter, *First Lady from Plains* (Boston: Houghton Mifflin, 1984), p. 357.

12 Their names are listed in Lu Ann Paletta, *World Almanac of First Ladies* (New York: World Almanac, 1990), p. 210.

13 Julia Dent Grant, *The Personal Memoirs of Julia Dent Grant* (Mrs. Ulysses S. Grant), ed. John Y. Simon (New York: G. P. Putnam's Sons, 1975), p. 18.

14 Barbara Bush, *A Memoir* (New York: Charles Scribner's Sons, 1994), p. 540.

PRESIDENTS' WIVES

First Lady	Lifespan	Husband	Years of Service	Married in
(Note: w=widowed, wa= widowed through assassination, d=died while First Lady)				
Martha Dandridge Custis Washington	1731–1802	George Washington	1789–1797	1759
Abigail Smith Adams	1744–1818	John Adams	1797–1801	1764
Dolley Payne Todd Madison	1768–1849	James Madison	1809–1817	1794
Elizabeth Kortright Monroe	1768–1830	James Monroe	1817–1825	1786
Louisa Catherine Johnson Adams	1775–1852	John Quincy Adams	1825–1829	1797
Anna Symmes Harrison	1775–1864	William H. Harrison	1841	1795
Letitia Christian Tyler	1790–1842	John Tyler	1841–1842[d]	1813
Julia Gardiner Tyler	1820–1889	John Tyler	1844–1845	1844
Sarah Childress Polk	1803–1891	James K. Polk	1845–1849	1824
Margaret Mackall Smith Taylor	1788–1852	Zachary Taylor	1849–1850[w]	1810
Abigail Powers Fillmore	1798—1853	Millard Fillmore	1850–1853	1826
Jane Means Appleton Pierce	1806–1863	Franklin Pierce	1853–1857	1834
Mary Todd Lincoln	1818–1882	Abraham Lincoln	1861–1865[wa]	1842
Eliza McCardle Johnson	1810–1876	Andrew Johnson	1865–1869	1827
Julia Dent Grant	1826–1902	Ulysses S. Grant	1869–1877	1848
Lucy Webb Hayes	1831–1889	Rutherford B. Hayes	1877–1881	1852
Lucretia "Crete" Rudolph Garfield	1832–1918	James A. Garfield	1881[wa]	1858
Frances "Frankie" Folsom Cleveland	1864–1947	Grover Cleveland	1886–1889,1893–1897	1886

Caroline Scott Harrison	1832–1892	Benjamin Harrison	1889–1893[d]	1853
Ida Saxton McKinley	1847–1907	William McKinley	1897–1901wa	1871
Edith "Edie" Kermit Carow Roosevelt	1861–1948	Theodore Roosevelt	1901–1909	1886
Helen "Nellie" Herron Taft	1861–1943	William Howard Taft	1909–1913	1886
Ellen Axson Wilson	1860–1914	Woodrow Wilson	1913–1914[d]	1885
Edith Bolling Galt Wilson	1872–1961	Woodrow Wilson	1915–1921	1915
Florence Kling Harding	1860–1924	Warren G. Harding	1921–1923[w]	1891
Grace Goodhue Coolidge	1879–1957	Calvin Coolidge	1923–1929	1905
Lou Henry Hoover	1874–1944	Herbert C. Hoover	1929–1933	1899
Anna Eleanor Roosevelt Roosevelt	1884–1962	Franklin D. Roosevelt	1933–1945[w]	1905
Elizabeth (Bess) Wallace Truman	1885–1982	Harry S Truman	1945–1953	1919
Mamie Doud Eisenhower	1896–1979	Dwight D. Eisenhower	1953–1961	1916
Jacqueline Bouvier Kennedy	1929–1994	John F. Kennedy	1961–1963wa	1953
Claudia "Lady Bird" Taylor Johnson	1912–	Lyndon B. Johnson	1963–1969	1934
Thelma Catherine "Pat" Nixon	1912–1993	Richard M. Nixon	1969–1974	1940
Elizabeth Betty Bloomer Ford	1918–	Gerald R. Ford	1974–1977	1948
Rosalynn Smith Carter	1927–	James E. Carter	1977–1981	1946
Nancy Davis Reagan	1923–	Ronald W. Reagan	1981–1989	1952
Barbara Pierce Bush	1925–	George Bush	1989–1993	1945
Hillary Rodham Clinton	1947–	William J. Clinton	1993–2001	1975

INDEX

GLOSSARY

bustle a cumbersome contraption of padding worn below the waist, at the back of a skirt, a fashion necessity for stylish women in the 1880s.

cabinet the heads of government departments and other important government officials.

calligraphers specialists in decorative handwriting.

chief of staff the official in charge of the president's or the First Lady's staff who supervises those in charge of scheduling, press releases, speechwriting, etc., who also serves as an advisor, and frequently controls access to his or her boss.

chief usher the individual in charge of overseeing the operation of the domestic White House staff and preparing the budget for the Executive Mansion.

conflict of interest competing demands of personal and professional life that might unduly influence the performance of official duties.

East Wing refers to the First Lady's staff, located in the East Wing of the White House, now known as the Office of the First Lady.

Equal Rights Amendment a proposed change in the Constitution that if approved by the states would have eliminated arbitrary distinctions based on gender.

etiquette the rules of proper social behavior.

franking the privilege of mailing letters free of charge by signing one's name in place of stamps.

front-porch campaigns a method of running for presidential office that had the candidates greeting visitors and giving speeches at home.

grand jury a group of citizens who determine whether formal charges should be brought against a person suspected of misconduct or criminal activities.

impeachment removal from office with a legislature acting as a court. In the case of a president of the United States, the House of Representatives brings formal charges after an investigation of the facts, and the Senate tries the case. A conviction in the Senate requires a two-thirds vote.

inauguration the ceremony swearing a president or governor into office.

National Security Council an advisory group to the president, charged with investigating and evaluating overseas threats to the United States.

nominating convention a meeting of delegates from all over the nation who choose the party's candidates for president and vice president and prepare the party platform.

patronage political favors such as appointing loyal individuals to government jobs and giving government contracts to wealthy contributors rather than subjecting them to competitive bidding.

platform committee an organization of political party members who prepare the party's stand on issues.

precedence rules determining who goes first during official ceremonies.

president elect a term used to refer to the winner of a presidential election who has not yet been sworn into office.

press secretary an aide to the president or the First Lady who handles their public image by releasing information to reporters and holding news conferences.

primary an election to determine a party's official candidate for office.

Prohibition a legal ban on the sale and manufacture of alcoholic beverages.

protocol rules of formal behavior.

rationing limiting supplies of scarce items, such as food and rubber, during wartime by issuing stamps periodically to all consumers that had to be turned in the items were purchased and were not easily replaced.

receiving line a formal method of greeting guests which requires them to file past a host and hostess when their name is announced, shake hands, and exchange a few words.

Social aides individuals who announce White House guests, converse, and dance with them.

social secretary the individual who advises the First Lady on her guest list, arranges for invitations to be sent, manages seating arrangements at White House functions, secures entertainers, and generally organizes festivities.

West Wing refers to the president's staff whose offices are located in the West Wing of the White House.

Women's Christian Temperance Union (WCTU) an organization that mobilized public opinion to condemn drinking liquor, beer, and wine and pressured Congress for a legal ban on the sale and manufacture of alcoholic beverages.

TO FIND OUT MORE

BOOKS

Boller, Jr., Paul F. *Presidential Wives: An Anecdotal History.* New York: Oxford University Press, 1988.

Caroli, Betty Boyd. *America's First Ladies.* Pleasantville, N. Y.: Reader's Digest Association, Inc., 1996.

First Ladies. New York: Oxford University Press, 1995.

Garrison, Webb. *A Treasury of White House Tales.* Nashville: Rutledge Hill Press, 1989.

Johnson, Haynes. *The Working White House.* New York: Praeger Publishers, 1975.

Klapthor, Margaret Brown. *The First Ladies.* Washington, D.C.: White House Historical Association, 1995.

Mayo, Edith P. and Denise Meringolo, *First Ladies: Political Role and Public Image.* Washington, D.C.: Smithsonian Institution, 1994.

Paletta, Lu Ann, *The World Almanac of First Ladies.* New York: World Almanac, 1990.

Skarmeas, Nancy. *First Ladies of the White House.* Nashville: Ideals Publications, Inc., 1995.

Smith, Nancy Kegan and Mary C. Ryan, eds. *Modern First Ladies: Their Documentary Legacy.* Washington, D.C.: National Archives and Records Administration, 1989.

Worth, Fred. L. *Fascinating Facts About Washington, D.C.* New York: Bell Books, 1988.

INTERNET SITES

National First Ladies' Library
http://www.firstladies.org/
This site was set up as "a unique, national resource for patrons from schoolchildren to serious scholars." It contains biographies and extensive bibliographies of the First Ladies.

The First Ladies of the United States of America
http://www2.whitehouse.gov/WH/glimpse/firstladies/html/first-
   ladies.html
This page provides a picture and short biography of each First
   Lady.

The White House
http://www.whitehouse.gov/WH/Welcome.html
The official site of the White House has links to various topics on White House history, First Ladies, and the United States government.

The First Lady of the United States
http://www.whitehouse.gov/WH/EOP/First_Lady/html/HILLARY_
   Home.html
Created and maintained by Hillary Rodham Clinton, this page offers Ms. Clinton's interesting commentary on her duties and ambitions as First Lady.

ABOUT THE AUTHOR

Barbara Silberdick Feinberg graduated with honors from Wellesley College where she was elected to Phi Beta Kappa. She holds a Ph.D. in political science from Yale University. Among her more recent works are *Watergate: Scandal in the White House, American Political Scandals Past and Present, The National Government, State Governments, Local Governments, Words in the News: A Student's Dictionary of American Government and Politics, Harry S. Truman, John Marshall: The Great Chief Justice, Electing the President, The Cabinet, Hiroshima and Nagasaki, Black Tuesday: The Stock Market Crash of 1929, Term Limits for Congress, The Constitutional Amendments, Next in Line: The American Vice Presidency,* and *Elizabeth Wallace Truman, Edith Kermit Carow Roosevelt,* and *Thelma Ryan Nixon,* in preparation. She has also written *Marx and Marxism, The Constitution: Yesterday, Today, and Tomorrow,* and *Franklin D. Roosevelt, Gallant President.* She is a contributor to *The Young Reader's Companion to American History.*

Ms. Feinberg lives in New York City with her two Yorkshire terriers, Katie and Holly. Among her hobbies are growing African violets and orchids, collecting antique autographs of historical personalities, listening to the popular music of the 1920s and 1930s, and working out in exercise classes.